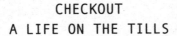

CHECKOUT
A LIFE ON THE TILLS

Anna Sam

Anna Sam was born in 1979 in Rennes where she still lives with her husband and two dogs. *Checkout: A Life on the Tills* is her first book.

Morag Young

Morag Young studied French and Italian at Leeds University and subsequently worked for the European institutions in Brussels and Strasbourg. She now lives in Paris and works as a translator.

CHECKOUT
A LIFE ON THE TILLS

CHECKOUT
A LIFE ON THE TILLS

ANNA SAM

Translated by Morag Young

Gallic Books

London

First published in France as *Les tribulations d'une caissière*
by Éditions Stock

Copyright © Éditions Stock, 2008
English translation copyright © Gallic Books 2009

First published in Great Britain in 2009 by Gallic Books,
134 Lots Road, London, SW10 0RJ

A CIP record for this book is available from the British Library

ISBN 978-1-906040-29-1

Typeset in Berkeley Book by SX Composing DTP, Rayleigh, Essex

Printed and bound by CPI Bookmarque, Croydon, CR0 4TD

2 4 6 8 10 9 7 5 3

*For my brother, Gwenael. I wish I could have
shared this book with you.
And for all those men and women
who have worked on the till.*

My name is Anna. I'm twenty-eight years old with a degree in literature and a life story that is both completely ordinary and a little bit unusual. I've worked for eight years in a supermarket. I started out there just to fund my studies and to have some financial independence. But when I couldn't find any work using my degree, I stayed on and became that stalwart of modern life, a checkout girl.

The till. Not a great conversationalist, unless you count the beeps it gives when you scan the produce. As a result of listening to that robotic noise I felt frankly that I was becoming a little like a robot myself. The fleeting interaction with the customers was not enough to make me feel human. Happily though, contact with my colleagues did just that.

One day I decided to write about my working life and record the little incidents that fill the day of a checkout girl. Suddenly I was looking differently at the customers filing past my till. I was seeing the world of retail with new eyes and discovering that it was a lot more varied than I had thought. There are the easy customers and the more challenging ones. Rich ones, poor ones. Nervous customers, boastful customers. Customers who treat you as if you were invisible and customers who say hello. The ones who are always champing at the bit for the store to open, and the ones who always come just as the store is closing. There are customers who flirt with you and customers who insult you. Who says nothing happens in the life of a cashier?

I wanted to share my experiences. I have put together here a few of my stories, the ones that affected me most. So it's time to take your trolley and come into the supermarket. Look, the shutters are already going up!

Happy shopping!

WELCOME TO THE WONDERFUL WORLD OF RETAIL - AND YOUR DREAM JOB

Congratulations! You've finally managed to get an interview and actually been hired. Welcome to the retail family. You are now a checkout girl . . . sorry, checkout *operator*. That feels much more important, doesn't it?

The interview only lasted a couple of minutes, long enough for you to repeat what's already on your CV and give them your bank details. No IQ tests? Or a bit of mental arithmetic? Come off it – you'll be suggesting they analyse your handwriting next. You're going to work on the till, you know, not being called to the Bar.

It's only your first day – but you still have to prove your worth. So let's get cracking, time for training. Don't worry though – an 'old hand' will take you under her wing for at least, I don't know, a quarter of an hour? A morning if you're lucky. Or two days if your manager is nice. There are some nice managers, I promise. It's just the luck of the draw.

Let's start with a tour of the store. It won't take long (and besides there are other things to be getting on with). There's only the locker room, the staff room, the waste disposal area with the bins where all the produce that's past its sell-by date ends up – you'll find you spend a lot of time here – the Office where you'll be given your float and . . . well, that's it.

Now you know enough about the store to get down to work. You'll have plenty of time to explore your new workplace further during your breaks. It will make them more fun.

The first time you approach the tills in your wonderful Chanel or Dior uniform, or your hideous overall (depending on the store and the kind of customers they want to attract) with your float under your arm (the equivalent of several days' salary no less) you are bound to feel a bit intimidated. Take a deep breath. That feeling will pass.

Right, you've found your till, organised your float and settled in. You're really concentrating and really motivated. The 'old hand' is beside you and you're all ears. You're ready to work. Not a moment too soon.

The main things to remember are: scan the items (with a quick glance to check that the price looks right), add up the total, tell the customer, ask for a loyalty card, take payment, give the customer their change, ask for ID if necessary and give them the receipt. All with a nice sincere smile. Of course. And then 'Thank-you-have-a-nice-day' and on to the next customer. Shall I go through it again?

To begin with it might seem that you have to work fast, too fast – especially if you start on a busy day. But it'll soon become automatic and you won't pay too much attention to what you're doing. Within a month it will be as if you and your till were one.

Time has flown by and the 'old hand' is already giving you less and less advice. It's all sinking in. You're becoming expert at scanning items and giving change. Well done! It's really not that complicated – you just need to know what to do when and the rest comes of its own accord.

Right, now the 'old hand' is leaving you to manage on your own. You'll be able to scan your first items independently. Hurrah! What a treat that will be.

Actually, apart from the *bee-eep* of the scanner, it's not very exciting . . . fortunately there's lots of interaction with customers (but be patient, more on that later).

Oh yes, I almost forgot. There's a part that's not that easy but, strangely, it's quite interesting. You have to learn all the code numbers by heart for items that are sold by the unit: lemons, peppers, garlic, artichokes, etc. Don't panic. There aren't that many and if you forget there is a prompt sheet on the till. And you can always ask your colleagues, Jessica, Emma, Kate, Sarah, who are never far away. Best not forget their names – not easy when you have about a hundred colleagues.

Your first day is almost over. The last customers are leaving and the store is closing. So what are your first impressions? Actually, it's quite a fun job. You scan lots of items (and discover things you didn't know how to use or even existed), you chat with people, you have pleasant colleagues, you listen to music all day and it's nice and warm.

A dream job. Well, almost. You have to come back and do it all again tomorrow. And the day after. And the day after that. And, as time goes by, getting up in the morning to go to your dream job won't be quite so appealing.

Believe me.

THE TOP 3 QUESTIONS ASKED
AT THE TILL

Pay attention please. This store's exclusive welcome gift to you is a set of the top three customer questions:

- 'Where are the toilets?'
- 'Don't you have any bags?'
- 'Are you open?'

Out of context they're not so bad. But wait until you're behind your till. By the end of the day these questions will make you want to commit an act of violence (or, at the very least, have a good scream). Judge for yourself.

The most urgent question: 'Where are the toilets?'

CUSTOMER (*rushing up and usually quite flustered*)
Where are the toilets?

CHECKOUT GIRL (*obliged to interrupt her conversation with another customer*)
Hello!

The customer does not reply.

CHECKOUT GIRL (*sighing but only inwardly*)
Over there.

And she points at the big glossy sign saying 'Toilets' hanging just opposite the tills. The customer rushes off. No 'thank you' or 'goodbye' or even 'damn it'. Takes too long. When you've got to go . . .

The most aggressive question: 'Don't you have any bags?'

One of this millennium's greatest revolutions is the disappearance of the complimentary plastic bags offered to customers by supermarkets. Some people find this very irritating, especially the first time they come across it.

They see it as a money-making scam. Their reasoning is as follows: 'If the store doesn't provide free bags any more, they can sell them to customers and boost their profits.' That thought had occurred to me too. But I also have the urge to say to my customers, 'Think about the future and all the beautiful countryside there will be without plastic. Isn't the sea a nicer place without bags floating in it?'

Now the disappearance of plastic bags is pretty much accepted. You no longer see irritated customers abandoning their overflowing trolleys at the till. Yes, that did used to happen. But you might still be lucky enough to experience the following:

CHECKOUT GIRL (*who has scanned the customer's three items*)
£2.56 please.

The customer pays by cheque (yes, really – he doesn't have any cash, you see).

CUSTOMER (*who is looking about at the end of the conveyor belt for bags for his pre-packaged tomatoes, his pre-packaged salad and his pre-packaged apples*)
Don't you have any bags?

CHECKOUT GIRL (*for the thirtieth time in less than two hours*)
Supermarkets don't provide plastic bags any more. There are boxes in the storeroom or we have recyclable bags for 10p, which can be exchanged when they wear out.

CUSTOMER (*furious, his eyes almost popping out of his head*)
Couldn't you have told me before I paid?

CHECKOUT GIRL (*sighing deeply but again only inwardly*)
Sorry, but we haven't provided bags for several months now. (*Smiling at the customer*) Why don't you just carry your shopping as it is? Everything is already wrapped in plastic.

Even more furious, the customer takes his apples and his salad . . . and departs minus his tomatoes. After all, he only has two hands.

The most annoying question: 'Are you open?'

So you aim to be the best, most polite, and friendliest checkout girl? OK, that's your right and it's very admirable (although don't forget how little you're paid). But promise

10

me that you will never let anyone address you as if you were your till. You are a human being, not a machine that beeps. It's not only customers who have rights. Here are a few suggestions as to how to deal with confused customers:

CUSTOMER
Are you open?

THE POLITE CHECKOUT GIRL
I'm not but my till is.

THE SARCASTIC CHECKOUT GIRL
Beeeeeep!

(*If the customer is really good-looking*)
Try me and see . . .

THE CHECKOUT GIRL WITH HER BEST SMILE
Are you?

I can't guarantee what reaction you'll get to any of the above.

Over time, you'll find that some customers vary the question:

- 'Are you closed?'
- 'Is she open?'
- 'Are you available?'
- 'Can I come over to you?'

It's up to you how you interpret them . . .

AN HAUTE COUTURE FASHION SHOW

Do you care about your appearance? Do you hate uniforms? I'm sorry to have to remind you then that even though checkout girls sit behind tills, that is not enough to identify them as checkout girls and so, to avoid any confusion, you have to wear a uniform. Anyway, how else would you feel like you were part of a big family, the big brand family of the chain you work for? Your uniform is essential if you are to give of your best.

Here are the various spring/summer/autumn/winter collections that await you.

The glamorous uniform

A suit with a skirt (generally navy blue) and flowery scarf

(*tastefully* poking out of the pocket of your jacket). Flat shoes to match your shirt (generally white) and to be bought with your own money. Did you dream of being an air hostess when you were little? If so, this outfit will make you feel your dream has been fulfilled. A budget airline though, I hope that's OK. You could also use it for a wedding, bar mitzvah or award ceremony (delete as necessary). Isn't life great?

Watch out though, don't make any abrupt movements. The stitches (made in China) are fragile and frankly the clothes aren't very well cut.

The grandma uniform

Do you need something to wear to put the bin out? Now you have just the thing, thanks to these wonderful shapeless black waistcoats and skirts or black pleated trousers size XXL. Even if you're only in your twenties, beware the attentions of the elderly. If you're hoping to attract customers under seventy, however, forget it, there's no chance. Oh and don't forget to have your knitting ready to complete the outfit.

Your queue will be the spiritual home of grannies.

The farmer's wife

This consists of an extra-large overall (colour ranging from electric blue to piglet pink) with poppers. Whether you're pregnant or not, people will assume you're eight months gone (or, if you're a man, that you're obese). Completely stain- and waterproof, so invaluable when it rains.

The clown costume

This one has a bright-red jacket over a shirt of a vile green, patterned with large flowers, and wide trousers of an indefinable colour. All that's missing for the Ronald McDonald look is the red nose. The customers certainly won't miss you. But you'll hope your friends will, so don't encourage them to stop by – you'll never hear the end of it.

The cheap uniform

Here we have a polo shirt, sleeveless waistcoat or T-shirt, made in Taiwan, and vaguely in the chain's colours (before washing, that is). This garb is worn by all employees of the store, regardless of their role. The stores that favour this style are experts at saving the pennies. Better hope it's one of these stores that offers you a job.

Besides, of all the options, you will look slightly less ridiculous in this one than in the others. I won't go any further than that. And the feeling of belonging to a big family will be even more pronounced.

Just to complete the fashion show, be aware that if you arrive at a bad time of year you might have to mix styles and find yourself wearing the Glamour/Clown, the Grandma/Farmer's Wife or the Clown/Grandma . . . Won't that be hilarious?

In any event, avoid looking at yourself too often in the mirror at work if you don't want to have a breakdown or be forced to resist the urge to laugh like a madman in front of every customer.

CASHING UP: THE SEARCH FOR
THE MISSING COIN

It is 9.05 p.m. That was your first real day. You have just served your last and 289th customer. You've been behind the till for eight hours with two fifteen-minute breaks. You're tired. You dream of one thing – going to bed and sleeping until 6 a.m. tomorrow.

Oi, wake up! The day isn't over yet!

You still have to clean your work station (you weren't naïve enough to think that a cleaner was going to do it for you, were you?) and cash up (you didn't have the cheek to think that you were being paid to do nothing, did you?). Count yourself lucky, at least here you don't have to clean the aisles.

Right, hurry up, over to the Office with your cash box!

Sit down over there with your colleagues and find a pen and paper. Don't yawn, you haven't finished work yet! Start by counting your coins, then your notes and finally your coin rolls. I say 'your' but obviously they're not really yours. Oh actually, count them in whatever order you please – you still have the right to make that choice. Don't let yourself be distracted by the chatter, the doors opening and closing and the rattling of coins. Concentrate or you'll regret it when you find yourself with the joy of recounting.

Not enough light? Don't complain, think of it as a relaxing soft light after the blinding glare of the store.

15 minutes later

OK, you have scrupulously noted how many 1p, 2p, 5p, 10p, 20p and 50p pieces, and £1 and £2 coins you have. And the number of £5, £10, £20 and £50 notes. And the number of coin rolls . . . Calm down, now. Yes, you have a small fortune in your hands. But don't think about that. Instead, think about your salary at the end of the month. That will bring you back down to earth again . . .

Add it all up and then subtract your till float (yes, the £150 in cash that was in your cash box at the start of the day).

'Right, 173, how much? 173?! Yes, that's you!'

'I have a name!'

'Yes, I know, but it's quicker this way. So, 173?'

'£3,678.65!'

'Count again, 173, you've made a mistake! I warned you. You weren't concentrating properly.'

'Am I way out? Or just a little? Under? Over?'

'Just count it again.'

10 minutes later

'£3,678.15!'

'OK. Before you go, check that your cheques and discount vouchers are safely put away. We're not your skivvies, you know.'

9.35 p.m. You take off your overall in the locker room. You only have five minutes to catch your bus. Good night and sweet dreams (full of *beeeep*s, hellos, goodbyes . . . perhaps not).

THE JOB INTERVIEW

I've forgotten to mention something very important about your job interview. I'll put that right straight away. It doesn't matter if you have never worked before, you don't know how to count, you are agoraphobic or afraid of the dark as long as you are available immediately, you accept the wonderful salary offered, you have a bank account and you can answer *this* question:

'Why do you want to work with us?'

Yes, even to be a checkout girl, you have to come up with a good reason.

Try one of the following:

'Because I've always dreamt of working in a supermarket!'

If you want them to believe you, say it with a *lot* of

conviction and make your eyes sparkle with enthusiasm at the same time. Not easy.

'Because my mother was a checkout girl!'

Same conviction and enthusiasm required as for the previous suggestion.

'Because like you I want to "make life taste better".' or 'Because, as you say, "Every little helps!"'

Stretching it a little, I know, but such devotion is always well received. So you might as well. You have to be careful though. Not all the slogans work. You might be wary of passing yourself off as 'Everyone's favourite ingredient'.

'I'm a student. I need a part-time job to support myself.'

The classic answer but very convincing. And managers really like students. They grumble less than old people and don't mind working at weekends. So it's an excellent answer. Of course, if you're not actually a student you have to look young enough to be credible. You shouldn't have too much of a problem up to the age of thirty or thirty-five.

'I need a job to survive.'

Avoid this answer – even if it's true, the manager will think you're 'not very motivated', 'lacking team spirit', 'unsuited to the store's commercial ambitions' and your application risks being relegated to the bottom of the pile (which is enormous, by the way).

But there are many answers that will impress. For inspiration pretend that you're applying to be a lawyer, instead of a checkout operator. Come on, use your imagination!

YOURS STATISTICALLY

Here are a few things to ponder if you are to be an unbeatable checkout girl:

- About 750,000 people work for supermarkets in the UK (you'll be joining a nice big family!).
- 15–20 items must be scanned every minute. This can increase to 45 at some discount chains. So the checkout girl has to handle customers' shopping without proper consideration, leading to damaged goods if customers can't keep up with the pace, which, of course, is nearly always the case. Well, they're not paid according to their performance – but neither is the checkout girl actually . . .
- 700 to 800 items scanned per hour.

- 21,000 to 24,000 items scanned per week.
- 800 kg of goods are lifted per hour (more than this on good days).
- 96 to 120 tonnes lifted per week (the equivalent of four HGVs!).
- Per year? Get out your calculator (not provided by your store).

Do I look like a bodybuilder? Well, hardly. Quite often I feel about seventy.

Every week you can consult the checkout-operator league table to find out who has taken the most money and whether you have been a tortoise or a hare. Don't panic. There's no reward (not even a bottle of ketchup) for the winner. But your parents and children will be really proud of you.

Every day you will say on average:

- 250 hellos
- 250 goodbyes
- 500 thank yous
- 200 'Do you have a loyalty card?'
- 70 'Please enter your PIN'
- 70 'Please take your card'

- 30 'The toilets are over there'

and many other similarly poetic lines.

You're not a robot, are you? Of course not! A robot doesn't smile.

- Your average monthly pay: £800 net.
- Hours worked a week: 30 (or 26, 24, 20 but rarely the full 35).

But let's get one thing straight. Don't think you'll be able to top up your hours with part-time work. Your manager will ensure that your rota will change every week. Of course you could always work as a cleaner from 5 a.m. until 8 a.m. or take in ironing. You didn't want any time for family, did you? Well done, you've chosen the ideal job.

Here's an example of a 30-hour week:

- Monday: 9 a.m. to 2.30 p.m. (working time: 5½ hours; break time: 16 minutes)
- Tuesday: rest day
- Wednesday: 3 p.m. to 8.45 p.m. (working time: 5 hours 45 minutes; break time: 17 minutes)
- Thursday: 1.45 p.m. to 5.15 p.m. (working time: 3½ hours; break time: 10 minutes)

- Friday: 3.15 p.m. to 9 p.m. (working time: 5 hours 45 minutes; break time: 17 minutes)
- Saturday: 9 a.m. to 1 p.m. / 3.30 p.m. to 9.15 p.m. (working time: 9 hours 45 minutes; break time: 12 minutes and 17 minutes)

And the following week? Don't worry, your hours will be completely different.

You'll be told your new schedule two weeks in advance, three weeks in advance if the person who creates the rota is particularly zealous, or twenty-four hours in advance if a lot of cashiers are away.

Six hours fifteen minutes is the maximum number of hours you can work on the till without a break (in theory, although some employment contracts contravene this).

You're entitled to three break minutes per hour worked, so if you want eighteen minutes to eat, you need to have worked at least six hours. You can forget about nice hot meals.

So there you have it. That's your dream job . . . is it all you hoped for? You have the supermarkets to thank for that.

'HANG ON A MINUTE, I'M AT THE CHECKOUT!'

Ah, mobile phones. What a marvellous invention. It's just incredible all the things they can do: play music, show TV, send emails, follow the stock market . . . Incidentally they also enable us to make calls when and where we want. But that's not all mobile phones can do. Some can even make a man (or a woman) invisible – and it's not only the most expensive models that can do it. The fact that checkout girls are pretty invisible anyway, helps with this trick.

> CUSTOMER (*on the phone, talking loudly as if he were on his own at home*)
> But I'm already at the till! Couldn't you have told me earlier that you wanted bananas?

CHECKOUT GIRL (*very loudly to remind him that he is at the till and not at home*)
Hello!

CUSTOMER (*apparently he still thinks he's at home*)
Go out tonight? Are you feeling better then?

CHECKOUT GIRL (*who has worked fast so that he soon will be at home*)
£13.50 please.

CUSTOMER (*collecting his shopping with one hand and not moving fast at all*)
I'm sure it's a stomach bug. I hope you haven't given it to me. I don't want to spend all night on the loo.

CHECKOUT GIRL (*getting up from her chair, clearing her throat, and speaking very loudly indeed*)
£13.50 please!

CUSTOMER (*with a quick glance at the checkout girl but continuing calmly to collect his shopping*)
. . . you're the one who never listens to me. You should wash your hands every time you go out.

CHECKOUT GIRL (*clenching her fists and speaking really, really loudly*)
Do you have a loyalty card?

CUSTOMER (*inserting his bank card into the machine without glancing up*)
. . . I get it, I'm not deaf. You're so grumpy when you're ill.

The customer grabs the receipt from the checkout girl's hand as if she were a ticket machine.

CUSTOMER (*moving away with his shopping, still on the phone and still talking loudly*)
. . . It's a good thing everyone's not like you.

CHECKOUT GIRL (*really loudly but only in her head*)
And it's a good thing everyone's not like you. What an idiot!

And she decides not to bother with a goodbye. Every small victory counts.

Don't feel sorry for yourself. You've just had an unforgettable experience – for a few minutes you have been completely invisible. And look on the bright side;

you might get to experience the same thing again but with a subtle difference.

CUSTOMER (*on the phone*)
Blah blah blah . . .

CHECKOUT GIRL
Hello!

CUSTOMER (*looking at the checkout girl*)
Hello. (*And eyes immediately focusing elsewhere*) So, as I was saying . . . blah blah blah . . .

I'm not exaggerating.

But there really is a reason to look on the bright side. It's not impossible that you will come across this rare specimen:

CUSTOMER (*on the phone*)
I'll call you back, I'm at the till.

The customer hangs up and puts his phone away.

CHECKOUT GIRL (*with a really big, sincere smile*)
Hello!

CUSTOMER (*returning her smile*)
Hello!

Isn't life great? Well yes, but don't get carried away. That kind of customer is very, very, very rare. People who have met them still talk about it . . .

Now, if you are particularly sensitive about appearing invisible and this is your second year behind the till (surely you're used to it by now?!) you might want to do this instead:

CUSTOMER (*on the phone*)
Blah blah blah . . .

CHECKOUT GIRL (*scanning products quickly while . . . talking on her hands-free kit*)
Blah blah blah . . .

CUSTOMER (*looking at the checkout girl*)
Don't you have any bags?

CHECKOUT GIRL (*without glancing at the customer*)
No. (*And immediately*) As I was saying, blah blah blah . . .

In your dreams – no, not even in your dreams. A checkout girl must always act like a checkout girl. And a checkout girl does not use the phone at work! At least not until computers have replaced her entirely. Some customers appear to think they already have.

ENTERTAINING THE SUPERMARKET

Another job which is almost as desirable as yours is the supermarket compere's. This strange specimen is wheeled out on very special occasions: Mother's Day, Grandparents' Day, Gardening Day, Green Plants Day, the First Day of Spring, the First Day of Summer, the First Day of Winter, Red Wine Day, White Wine Day, Beer Day, Pork Pie Day, Scotch Egg Day, Salmon Day, Chocolate Cake Day, etc. You'll soon learn that any occasion is a good excuse for a party. And on those days how you will regret not being a customer. All those special offers and presents galore you will miss out on . . .

And you will very soon realise that not just anyone can be a supermarket compere.

You need a nice voice (well, a voice) and a *lot* of

endurance. Supermarket comperes have to be able to talk into their microphone almost all day without stopping (which will rapidly make you detest them).

They also have to be convincing.

COMPERE (*into the microphone*)
Ladies and gentlemen, today we have a wonderful, magnificent, sublime, gigantic special offer: buy two sausages and get the third free! Wonderful value if you're planning a superb, magnificent family barbecue!

And they must be good at the schmaltz.

COMPERE
. . . Ah, a family barbecue . . . What could be nicer than a family barbecue? What could be more touching? So don't forget, tomorrow is Mother's Day. Do something nice for Mum! For only £2.54!

They must enjoy travel.

COMPERE
I am currently in the bread-products aisle. Come and join me as we taste French pastries, lovingly made by artisans: croissants, *pains au chocolat*,

pains aux raisins, just some of their specialities!

They have to have the charm of Chris Tarrant (generally they think they *are* Chris Tarrant).

COMPERE (*to a customer*)
So, madam, what is the capital of France? Paris, Berlin or Madrid? The right answer will win you this wonderful, amazing, magnificent barometer . . .

CUSTOMER
Um, I don't know.

COMPERE
Do you want to phone a friend? (*The compere laughs heartily as he says this – comperes also need a sense of humour.*)

CUSTOMER
OK.

COMPERE
OK, I'm your friend. Here's a clue: it starts with 'P'.

CUSTOMER
Peterborough!

COMPERE (*surprised*)
Uh . . . no. The answer was Paris. But never mind,
madam. Since it's Mother's Day tomorrow, you
win this wonderful, amazing, magnificent bouquet
of flowers!

And finally they need to be resourceful.

COMPERE (*into the microphone*)
Little Johnny has lost his mum and dad. Could
they come quickly to the pet-food aisle. Their little
boy really needs to go to the loo!

So you see, it's true. Not everyone has the skills to be
a supermarket compere. You will come to admire them
for their ability to make so much of so little. It's a high-
wire act!

Hats (and microphones) off to them.

I'VE SAVED A PLACE

Some people have a real phobia about queuing. But how can you avoid it at the supermarket, or the post office for that matter? With subtle little ploys, that's how. Here are the most devious.

Tactic 1

> DEVIOUS CUSTOMER (*running up with four items in his hand*)
> Are you open?
>
> CHECKOUT GIRL
> I'm not but my till is! Hello!

DEVIOUS CUSTOMER
Excellent!

The customer's four items are scanned.

CHECKOUT GIRL
£5.45 please.

DEVIOUS CUSTOMER
Hang on, my girlfriend's just coming – she forgot something.

Five minutes later, still no girlfriend in sight and the queue of customers is building up behind him.

CHECKOUT GIRL (*sensing the mounting tension*)
Can I ask you to wait to one side?

DEVIOUS CUSTOMER (*who's oblivious to the tension but is annoyed by the question*)
She's coming! Can't you wait just a second?

And indeed at that moment the checkout girl sees her arrive with . . . two baskets filled to the brim.

CUSTOMER BEHIND THE DEVIOUS CUSTOMER
Don't mind me!

The checkout girl privately thinks the waiting customer is right to be aggrieved.

DEVIOUS CUSTOMER
I queued too, you know, like everyone else!

Tactic 2

The devious customer runs up with her trolley and starts to empty it on to the conveyor belt.

CHECKOUT GIRL
Hello!

But the devious customer has already disappeared, leaving her trolley still half full. The checkout girl tells herself that she'll be back in a minute and starts scanning the items on the conveyor belt. Another customer arrives.

CHECKOUT GIRL (*conciliatory*)
Hello, the person in front of you will be back in just a minute.

The other customer sighs. Two minutes later there is still no sign of the first customer.

CUSTOMER 2 (*not happy*)
I've got other things to do, you know!

CHECKOUT GIRL (*embarrassed*)
She'll be right back, I promise.

Two minutes later, still no one.

CUSTOMER 2 (*aggressive*)
This is beyond a joke!

CHECKOUT GIRL (*very, very embarrassed*)
I'm sorry.

CUSTOMER 2
Sorry! Well, that's not good enough. I'm changing tills. It's outrageous!

And the second customer changes tills just as the devious customer calmly returns with her arms full.

DEVIOUS CUSTOMER
If I'd known you had no one waiting I wouldn't
have rushed!

Tactic 3

The checkout girl has no one at her till and indicates to an
elderly customer waiting nearby that she should come to
her till. The customer hurries over as fast as she is able
and when she is almost there, a man rushes up and does
a flashy fishtail move with his trolley. He immediately
starts putting his shopping on the conveyor belt.

CHECKOUT GIRL
Excuse me, sir, this lady was here before you.

DEVIOUS CUSTOMER (*without so much as a glance at
the lady in question*)
You're joking! Hurry up, I haven't got all day.

The elderly customer indicates to the checkout girl
that it doesn't matter. Shame . . .

Tactic 4

The checkout girl serves several customers and then turns to find an empty trolley without an owner. Five other customers are waiting behind.

> CHECKOUT GIRL (*to the customer behind the empty trolley*)
> Come past please.

As the checkout girl is serving the third customer in line, the owner of the empty trolley rushes up with two bags full of shopping and unhesitatingly pushes in front.

> THIRD CUSTOMER
> Excuse me but I was here before you!

> VERY DEVIOUS CUSTOMER (*pointing at the empty trolley*)
> Excuse me but *I* was here before *you*!

If the third customer decides not to let this go the atmosphere will turn ugly very quickly. Abuse will fly and a fight could break out. And frankly, the very, very devious customer has behaved so badly that you'd have to be a saint to stay calm.

The checkout girl, with the best seat in the house, keeps score and leaves them to get on with it.

I would advise all these very devious customers to do their shopping on the Internet. They will find it less tiring than treating everyone else like idiots . . .

KISSING COUPLES

So you thought supermarkets weren't the sexiest of places? Think again.

They are much more erotic places than you had imagined. You'll be surprised how many kisses are stolen in the aisles (including in the loo-roll aisle . . .), by the number of languorous glances exchanged between the butcher's counter and the fishmonger's, by the number of hands on bottoms in the frozen-food section, of breasts (and more if the chemistry is right) caressed in the lingerie aisle, and by the romantic and even passionate conversations in front of the cheese counter. You'll be surprised as well by the number of domestic disputes . . .

Why? Maybe the plethora of products all within arm's reach excites the senses.

Once it was my good fortune to witness real passion. It was the end of the day. Most people had gone. There was no one at my till (yes, it does happen). I was looking around (I know, the till won't clean itself) and my glance fell on a couple and their four children in the comics aisle. I was immediately struck by the great tenderness between Mum and Dad and I said to myself that to be so in love after four children was the stuff of dreams.

And I starting daydreaming at my till . . . lots of romantic images passed through my mind until a sound like the unblocking of a sink made me look up. My dream couple were walking towards me with their trolley and four children . . . and snogging. Hence the romantic noise.

I told myself that love is deaf as well as blind. And can't afford to wait either. All the time they were at my till they were fondling each other. And completely without inhibition either – they weren't worried about anyone catching sight of Mum's pink lacy G-string or Dad's very hairy bum. Their children, unmoved, left them to it and took care of packing the shopping. I suppose it's better than parents who argue. But I have to admit I blushed. It's not every day that passion is aroused in front of your till.

But in your role as hostess of this love shack you should expect to inspire desire too (even though your uniform is horrible). Be prepared for these grand declarations of love:

CHECKOUT GIRL
£65.78 please. Do you have a loyalty card?

CUSTOMER (*enterprising*)
Do you want to sleep with me tonight?

Others will be slightly less direct, a little shyer and a bit more obsessive too. They will come to your till nineteen times in one week, each time with just one item. Eyes always on the floor. No hello or goodbye. You'll start wondering if they're a bit mad. But on the twentieth occasion:

CUSTOMER (*white as a sheet*)
Could . . . could I . . . I . . . buy you a drink?

If you say no you'll break his heart but save your own . . . The rejected admirer will generally run away without asking for his change. And you stand there with your mouth open, taken aback by the turn of events.

Exciting, isn't it?

And love at first sight? Perhaps, you might be lucky . . . but let me remind you: you're a checkout girl and this isn't a Hollywood movie.

'EMBARRASSING' ITEMS

What embarrasses or intimidates customers? Surely nothing, you say – isn't that the nature of customers? Well, let me put you straight because there are a few items that bother some customers. And thanks to these items you get a little insight into those dear customers' personalities. How you will laugh, but only inside.

Loo roll

Everyone uses it (consumption in Britain is more than twice the European average). And yet, for some customers it's as if their loo roll smells bad already. You barely have time to scan it (don't be sadistic and pretend you can't find the bar code) before they grab it from you and bury it at the bottom of their trolley or bag under their other shopping. They will only breathe easy again once they are sure 'it' can't be seen. And if 'it' can still be seen (because the bag is too small or the 32-roll family pack is too large), they will try their best for several seconds to push 'it' out of sight. Others will desperately try to find brochures and leaflets to cover it. And they will all scuttle away from your till as quickly as possible.

Sanitary towels

Apparently, for some girls (and even those who aren't girls any more) periods are still a shameful illness. Luckily, sanitary-towel packaging and tampon boxes are more discreet than loo roll and can quickly be stowed in bags. However, not before you've seen these customers blush furiously, mumble an embarrassed 'hello', their eyes on their shoes, and drop their change in their nervousness. It's as if you had suddenly become a very imposing person. Amazing, a checkout girl can actually intimidate her customers! And then there are those for whom it is such an insurmountable ordeal that they prefer to send their husband or boyfriend to buy them. And generally these men find it rather amusing. You will be surprised by how often that happens.

But you shouldn't be surprised by any of this. When

you think of all the adverts that systematically highlight bad smells and leaks, which will make everyone look at you, it's no wonder that some people feel ashamed.

Condoms (my favourite 'embarrassing' item)

There are, of course, the customers who appear to think, 'If I hide this condom, no one will see it.' They try to 'drown' the box in amongst other items (some will even make sure that they choose other products whose colour and packaging are similar to the condom packet's), or they throw it down on the conveyor belt at the last minute like a casual afterthought. But they should beware of throwing it too hard because it might end up on the conveyor belt of the till next door where their neighbour is just paying for her shopping. If that happens their only recourse is to move to South America . . .

Then there are customers who don't give a damn. But they aren't funny.

And there are the show-offs. Real comedians. Pumped full of testosterone, they put two or even three or four boxes of XXL condoms on the conveyor belt. They don't buy anything else, obviously, unless it's lubricating jelly . . . and they fully expect all the customers around them (and preferably the whole shop) to notice and look at them with admiration (if they're ladies) and jealousy (if they're men). They won't appreciate it if you scan their boxes too quickly but will love you if you use your microphone to ask the price (specifying that it's XXL). And obviously they never use a bag.

Erotic films

As you would expect, when the show-off buys one he places it proudly with his boxes of condoms. The more hardcore the title, the happier he is.

Then you get the couple who find it 'scandalous' that 'you' (obviously it's always your fault when things go wrong) don't sell porn. But this shouldn't happen too often. Supermarkets today have understood that porn is a juicy market and often have a designated aisle. Yes, they are hidden in the corner, right at the top, out of reach of children . . .

But others try to be more discreet.

They purchase their porn film with other, more 'family-oriented' films (Walt Disney, for example) and sandwich it between two others when it comes to paying (as if to say 'How did that get there?'). Cinderella appears to have increased her bra size recently, you think . . .

They ask for it to be gift-wrapped every time they buy one. Probably to give it to their wives instead of flowers. Or for a couple of friends who are going through a rough patch. Or because there are no more plastic bags. You will be dying to ask them which one it is.

You will also see husbands who only buy them when they are alone and only pay in cash.

And of course, not to mention (OK, I will then) the customer whose DVD doesn't scan properly so that everyone can hear you ask, 'DVD aisle please, Till 5 would like to know the price of *Debbie Does Dallas*.' And I'd like to see the expression on your face when that happens.

Ah, so many unforgettable experiences await you!

I'M HUNGRY!

At lunchtime you often see customers using their lunch break to do their shopping but you also see others (and it could be the same ones) just tucking in there and then. The supermarket starts to look like a self-service café. And some customers a little like pigs.

Maybe it could be a new retail concept.

Imagine having this lot at your till:

Customer 1: He's in the process of devouring his tuna and mayo sandwich – noisily with his mouth wide open so that you can see everything inside (hey, where are the gherkins?). You ask him if you can borrow his sandwich for a second to scan the price. You have to wait for him to bite another piece off before he hands it to you and he

52

takes it back almost immediately. Mind your fingers. He pays and thanks you with some incomprehensible words accompanied by pieces of tuna and bread which land on your conveyor belt. Wonderful, you get to use your paper towel and cleaning products sooner than you'd planned. But watch out: mayonnaise is slippery.

Customer 2: He puts his items on your belt, including a packet of crisps, which you pick up. They spray all over your till because he hasn't thought it necessary to warn you that he has already opened the packet. On the other hand, he does find it necessary to shout at you (just what you need) and demand another packet of crisps. While he goes to get them, best to give your till a quick clean. And never mind if your hands are all greasy, they'll go with your conveyor belt which is already well coated.

Customer 3: You've noticed him in the queue and already feel ill. You've seen him unwrap a family-sized Camembert and bite straight into it. When it's his turn he has already finished it. How can he have gobbled it all down at such speed? The smell is making you gag. And it will hang around long after the customer has gone.

Customer 4: This one shouts at you because you want to make her pay for the bottle of fruit juice she drank and left beside the till. It's true of course and you should never forget it: checkout girls are meant to be blind and stupid.

The lunch period requires nerves of steel *and* a strong stomach. But you'll soon get used to it and the sight of customers who eat in the aisles will no longer revolt you. One less thing to scan, you'll tell yourself.

Is it time for your lunch now? *Bon appétit!*

MONEY-BACK GUARANTEE –
A VERITABLE GOLD MINE!

I admire those customers (mostly female) who only buy the store's bargains and nothing else. Maybe it's their revenge for ever-rising prices and the feeling that they are being squeezed dry.

This kind of customer has an iron will. She has a long detailed shopping list and never allows herself to be tempted by anything that is not on special offer. Standing in front of the cheese counter, she would like to buy Camembert, but only Roquefort is covered by the money-back guarantee. Neither she nor her husband like it much but never mind, she takes it anyway. Four of them. Same thing for the fruit yoghurts – only the strawberry flavour is eligible for the refund guarantee and her son hates strawberry. She gets it anyway. 'Strawberry flavour or no pudding.'

She also plans ahead: the family-sized washing powder – 'Not satisfied? Money-back guarantee.' Five packets. 'It will always come in handy. There are three of us at home.' The same thing for the flour – thirty points on your loyalty card. Ten packets. 'There'll be some left over for Christmas.' (Even though it's only January.)

Finally, this type of customer has a lot of patience. On each trip, she meticulously checks all round the store to make sure she doesn't miss any bargains. But it's at the till that she really needs patience. She will require a receipt for every item covered by the money-back guarantee as proof of purchase. You do the maths: thirty items, thirty receipts and about fifteen minutes' patience (and more if she pays by card, cash, cheque and voucher, and alternates payment methods).

And when this bargain hunter comes to *your* till you're always a bit nervous. Is she nice? Does she know her way around the system? Otherwise, she might wait until you've scanned all the items (35), told her the total amount due (£52.38), asked for a loyalty card (twice because she didn't answer the first time) before saying 'Oh, I need a separate receipt for each item!'

So what if lots of people are waiting? That's not her problem. All the bargain customer wants is those infamous receipts, the open sesame for the money-back guarantee.

Luckily, the regulars come at quiet times and love sharing their discoveries with the checkout girls.

And bargain customers must be very good cooks. Making something every day out of sardines in oil ('30 points on your loyalty card') and cheese-flavoured crisps ('Win a trip to Center Parcs'), or coffee ('3 for the price of 4') and tomato sauce ('45% free') is not easy. And spaghetti hoops ('money-back guarantee!') eight times a month is nice but won't you get tired of it the following month?

THE WONDERFUL LOYALTY CARD IN
ALL ITS COMPLICATED SIMPLICITY

What's the point? There isn't one, or not much of one (don't kid yourself – it won't make you a millionaire). It's just an ingenious way to encourage customers to come back to a particular store instead of going to their competitors. Yes, you can win a cuddly toy with 3,000 points (1 point for every pound spent in store), a darts board with 5,000 points, a plastic fruit-bowl with 10,000 points, a trip to Eurodisney in the raffle, a portable DVD player (that breaks after a week) with 90,000 points and £25 or a gift voucher worth £5 which is only valid for special offers . . . Really makes you want to fight tooth and nail to get that supermarket loyalty card, doesn't it? And makes it imperative that you go out and buy as many products as possible as often as possible.

But that's just scratching the surface of what the loyalty card can give you. It also offers amazing vouchers: 50p for a box of washing powder worth £9.98 or a refund for one item if you buy five others the same – as long as you have the card and come back and spend the amount you won in the store the next day (I always admire the simplicity of their explanations, don't you?). Then there are the special-offer days when cardholders (aren't they lucky?) can buy more to spend more.

But never, ever forget the expiry date for your precious points or your voucher because, if you go over the expiry date, you will lose all the benefits you have stored up with such effort over the months or even years and you can kiss goodbye to that pack of playing cards, that synthetic teddy bear or that fondue set . . .

I admire the way the marketing people in super-markets so readily (or should that be so disdainfully?) assume that their customers will react to loyalty cards like children who have been presented with a Kinder Surprise. But, given the success of loyalty cards, consumers do seem to have rediscovered their inner child. And today 'the card' is essential. The more you have (any of them), the more you feel the company belongs to you. But above all, if we didn't have loyalty cards the checkout girls wouldn't have anything to say to the customer. ('How does it work?' 'Why doesn't it give me anything?' 'How many points do I have?' 'Will my Club Card work at Sainsbury's?' 'I didn't have my card with me last month – can you add my points?' and so on.) That really would be a shame.

CLOSING TIME AND OPENING TIME – WHAT FUN!

'We would like to inform customers that the store will be closing in fifteen minutes. Please make your way to the tills. Have a nice evening.'

8.45 p.m.: Panic buying. Customers go mad. There's not a minute to lose. People start running all over the place.

And bang! Trolleys collide with each other.

Crash! The chocolate-box pyramid falls down.

'Damn it, they've already packed up the green beans!'

Thud! Chuck the butter, milk, cheese and yoghurts in the trolley . . . and never mind the rest.

'Why are they closing so early? Lazy so and sos!'

8.55 p.m.: The music from the speakers stops.

'Quick, get to the till!'

Only three tills still open. A few minutes to wait in the queue. 'You'll have time to get some pasta while I wait!'

9 p.m.: The security grating at the entrance starts to close.

Right, the last customer has gone through. Oh no! Here's another one running over, out of breath.

The lights start to go out.

That's it, the day really is over.

You let out a little sigh of relief, followed almost immediately by a cry of amazement. Who is that in the biscuits aisle? There's a trolley, right at the end . . . a couple is wandering up as if they have all the time in the world. You can tell from their attitude that they don't intend to head to the tills yet. But sparks are going to fly – the security guard has spotted them too.

But no! He's the one who is shouted at. The couple get angry. You can hear raised voices. The lady's face is all red.

After a good five minutes the argument stops and the couple follow the security guard, irritated. You think he's won. But suddenly, when they are only a few feet away from your till, the husband turns around and dashes back to get that packet of biscuits. A matter of life or death, apparently. The woman continues to push her trolley slowly, looking you straight in the eyes.

Their time at the till is spent being slow and verbally abusive.

One item scanned, one insult thrown at you ('It's a scandal, we're your best customers. We have the right to take our time to choose!'). One item scanned, one insult thrown at you ('Don't go so fast, are you stupid or something?'). One item scanned, one insult thrown at you . . . And their trolley is full.

9.25 p.m.: The couple leave your till. All the lights are out except yours, like a lighthouse fighting the wind and waves. You have been on overtime for twenty-five minutes. It's unpaid but you can claim it back in leave when management feels like it. Smile – the couple come back at least twice a month and always at the same time. But hey, the next time they come at closing time you won't be there, it'll be your day off, you lucky thing!

I have one piece of advice: buy a punchball!

But isn't life great? There is also an opening-time version of this couple. And the countdown starts early!

8.25 a.m., 35 minutes before opening: Their car arrives in the car park. They are the first. They beam with pride.

They can park in the best place, just in front of the entrance. The first victory of the day. Quick, there's no time to lose: get the best trolley (sparkling clean inside and with no squeaky wheels).

30 minutes before opening: They are in position, the front of their trolley is touching the entrance barrier. It has started to rain. They have forgotten their umbrella. But they won't wait in the car and risk having their place stolen when a second car arrives! The second victory of the day.

15 minutes before opening: They are soaked through but still the first of more than . . . six people. So that makes six victories so far. Their impatience and adrenaline mount. Their trolley revs as they do a final check of the shopping list with simultaneous visualisation of the store's aisles. Once inside they mustn't lose a second. Careful! Raindrops are smudging the shopping list. Never mind, they know it by heart.

5 minutes before opening: Your day begins. A big sigh followed by a long yawn. Your eyes are still puffy with sleep. You sit down with your cash box. You glance at the entrance and notice the seven . . . eight . . . ten . . . fifteen morning fanatics. You let out another big, long sigh.

1 minute before opening: The couple are dripping wet. 'It's always the same at this shop, they always open late!'

Opening time: 'Good morning and welcome to . . .' The noise of the security grating rising prevents the end of the welcome message being heard.

The couple: 'Ah, at last!' And the grating rises and rises . . . slowly, too slowly. They slip underneath. The security guard indicates that they should wait. 'You're late, we've got other things to do, you know!' they say, angry.

Opening time + 30 seconds: Right, they have (finally!) got through the door, the first to do so. There's not a second to lose. They head straight to the meat aisle. There won't be enough for everyone.

Opening time + 4 minutes: They are your first customers. And you record the first *beeeep!* of the day. Well done! You're impressed: thirty items collected in less than five minutes. That's a first. You watch them. They must be savouring their absolute victory. Well, no actually. The husband is annoyed. 'Can't you go a bit faster?'

Opening time + 7 minutes: They leave your till. With a 'thank you' or 'goodbye'? Anything? No time . . . the exit is at the other end of the store.

Opening time + 8 minutes: The exit security grating is not open yet. The couple are standing in front of it, furious. That makes your day.

Opening time + 30 minutes: They have gone home. They have put their shopping away. Their hair is still wet. And they have nothing else planned for the day. The husband sneezes . . . Outside the rain has stopped . . . The sun comes out.

So which would you prefer, the Opening Time couple or the Closing Time couple? Can't decide? How about both in the same day?

WHAT A COMEDIAN

Until now I haven't given you a very positive image of customers. Let me put that right straight away by telling you about the ones who make you laugh. Hold on to your till, it's going to be great.

In the space of one day on average you will hear:

'Am I disturbing you?' (18 times)
18 times a day you'll reply, 'No rest for the wicked!'

17 times a day you'll hear, 'Were you waiting for me?'
17 times a day you'll reply, 'Of course, I was starting to get worried!'

15 times you'll hear, 'If I'm nice will you give me a good price?'

15 times you'll reply, 'Do you want it twice or three times as expensive?'

10 times you'll hear, 'It's free then!' (because the price won't scan).

10 times you'll reply, 'Of course it is, take the trolley as well.'

8 times you'll hear, 'I've packed my shopping. Can I leave without paying?'

8 times you'll reply, 'If you run fast!'

Once you'll be asked, 'What d'you call a camel with three humps?'

Once you'll reply (even if you know the answer off by heart), 'I don't know, what *do* you call a camel with three humps?'

Once the customer will answer 'Humphrey!'

Once someone will try to do an impersonation of a celebrity.

Once you'll reply (in good faith), 'The Queen?'

Once the customer will reply, disappointed, 'No, Bruce Forsyth!'

Don't look like that! At least they aren't nasty, and actually acknowledge your presence. OK, being treated like an idiot isn't great. But if you don't answer, at least give them a little smile (I know, it'll encourage them to do it again next time).

And by the way, do you know what the checkout girl's best feature is? It's her laugh!

A HEALTHY MIND IN A HEALTHY BODY

Ladies and Gentlemen, are you fed up with your unsightly spare tyres? Do you dream about losing your love handles? Are you finding it impossible to reach your ideal weight?

Panic over – by working on the till you have chosen the best possible path to weight loss. The miracle solution is at the end of the conveyor belt.

Let the Checkout Girl and Body™ laboratory guide you: follow these exercises and your well-being will improve in record time.

Lose weight

Your shifts will change every day and from one week to the next. The upside: you'll skip meals, leading to certain weight loss. Checkout Girl and Body™ has proved it. Small downside: you must avoid snacking during your breaks. If the snack machine in the staff room makes eyes at you it'll quickly give you some extra padding which will keep you warm but will be fatal for your dream body! But your limitless willpower will keep you away from these servants of the devil and point you in the healthy direction of a bottle of mineral water (or tap water) and apples, your only indispensable workplace companions. Small downside: the noise of your stomach could rival the beep of your till. Never mind, you can always put it down to stress.

Work those biceps

Ah, blessed be the stores which require you to lift heavy items on to the till to be scanned. Thanks to this additional effort when you work on the till you will be able to tone your arms beautifully. Your biceps will be endlessly grateful for these relentlessly repeated exercises. Be sure to keep up a good pace!

Small downside: Checkout Girl and Body™ has not been able to determine whether carrying heavy items can create tendonitis. Some checkout girls regularly complain of this but Checkout Girl and Body™ wonders whether this is not just pure fabrication.

Do you dream of having beautiful buns?

No problem, your position when you're working (half sitting, half standing) will tone your thighs and buttocks. Aren't you lucky! And don't forget, for the best results get up and sit back down thirty or forty times an hour. This is very do-able during your working time and you will change your shape with grace and flexibility. Checkout Girl and Body™ has proved it.

Small downside: it appears (but again this has not been proved by our laboratory) that this kind of exercise can lead to various kinds of backache. Checkout girls who have not agreed to be examined by the Checkout Girl and Body™ doctors have claimed that they suffer from sciatica and lumbago. But that's just rumour at the moment . . .

Get firmer breasts!

Yes! As amazing as it sounds, the job of checkout girl has a big advantage for you, ladies! You carry a variety of heavy objects and you rotate by nearly 120 degrees with these items, which tones your pectorals. The result will be visible after only a few weeks. Your breasts will be firmer!

It's easy to compare yourself with women who aren't as lucky as you. A customer passes by? A new checkout girl arrives? Look at her chest area and then look at yours, which already has several months' work behind it. Can't you see a clear difference?

Checkout Girl and Body™ has proved it, checkout girls have nice firm chests. No more droopy boobs!

Small downside: there is a slight risk of straining your back and this exercise is, of course, better suited to women. Some men might have to wear bras after a few months. But you have to admit it's worth it!

Develop your immune system

Before working on the till, did you get colds, sore throats and flu all the time? Permanent contact with customers (one in seven will be carrying a virus during epidemics like gastroenteritis) will strengthen your immune system and make you resistant to all illnesses. What's more, by working near the freezers, automatic doors which are nearly always open and air conditioning, you will become stronger in the long term.

Small downside: it appears that some employees will become more receptive to viruses because of prolonged contact with all these germs. A study is in progress but there's no need to panic. Checkout Girl and Body™ suspects that some staff have started this rumour as an excuse to blow their noses at the till in front of customers.

Learn to put your make-up on

Sitting behind a till all day under fluorescent lights will cause your complexion to lose its natural sparkle. Not a problem – after a few months' work you will have become an expert in applying foundation (not provided by the store) to put some sparkle back into your grey skin. And use your breaks to get some sun in the store's (noisy and polluted) car park. The reflection of rays on the cars will make you brown (or baked) in record time.

Give your brain a break

Note too that, with regard to the state and development of your brain, the automatic movements and phrases repeated a thousand times a day will allow your mind to take a break during your working day. You can engage your brain again when you leave the shop. A good way of preserving your neurones for when you're old.

Small downside: some customers will confuse you with a house plant or the village idiot. Let them, it makes them feel superior and they will be delighted to come back and do their shopping with you. You have won your first regular customers. Checkout Girl and Body™ is proud of you!

So, dear customers, next time you do your shopping take a look at the checkout girls and observe the secret moves they use every day to create their dream bodies.

Working on the till is even better than going to the gym! Right, bring on the water bottles and cat litter!

SIT DOWN IF YOU CAN

You know the children's game, Musical Chairs? Did you like it when you were little? That's all right then, you're in luck! Your store's management lets you play it again but especially on Saturdays and the day before bank holidays. So how is the game played? It's very easy.

Saturday morning, about 11.30 a.m. You reach your till, happy to have a new day of work before you and, oh joy, you discover that there's no chair.

And so it begins.

Agitated, you glance right and left. The thirty tills are operating, their lights are all on. Have you already lost? A big sigh. But no, there is hope, twelve tills away the light is out. You take to your heels and off you fly. But what a disappointment! Your colleague has just forgotten to put the light on. What an idiot! You're about to say so when you see another empty till and an empty chair! You check, no, it's not a mirage, they are both empty. Isn't life great? You make for the empty till. Your heart is beating hard and you throw yourself on the chair.

Have you won? Not yet. You have to get it back to your till as quickly as possible. If you're absent for more than five minutes, with or without a chair, you've lost. And you only have two minutes left.

Bother, the chair is too big for the gap! Come on, clumsy, pull on it with all your strength! Damn, it doesn't have wheels. And it's really heavy!

Stop moaning, pick it up and hurry! You only have a minute left and seventy metres to go. Do you give up? Perhaps you'd rather pull it because of your lumbago? OK, but you've lost anyway and the squeaking of the chair's wheels is giving you away . . . Oops, sorry, you've hit a customer's trolley . . . OK, you've finally reached your till? At last!

Are you sweating profusely and thinking you can get your breath back? Well, think again and get to work. At least 350 customers to serve during the day and five are already waiting (crafty ones . . . they were following you while you hunted for a chair). There's not a moment to lose. You can get your breath back at your next break.

But why, you ask, wasn't there a chair at your till?

Answer: there used to be enough chairs for everyone but it would be too easy just to replace every broken one, and, anyway, it's a fun game, isn't it?

THOU SHALT NOT STEAL

Supermarkets – veritable treasure troves but, unfortunately, everything has to be paid for. Sometimes, though, especially if your purse is empty, or you're a kleptomaniac, the temptation to steal is just too strong. It's only human. But if you don't want to get caught, dear customer, avoid the following ploys, which are all too well known by checkout girls, or else make sure you perfect them.

The smooth talker

This ploy involves being very voluble. The customer relates their life story and tells lots of jokes with extravagant gestures. This customer is a real clown – actually, a real magician. They hope to distract the checkout girl's attention so that she won't notice that underneath their coat their stomach is strangely round.

Do you have the gift of the gab like Graham Norton or Russell Brand? Give it a go but you must be sure you have the necessary talent, otherwise your next performance will be in front of a couple of police officers . . .

The arguing couple

While the checkout girl scans their items a sudden violent argument breaks out between husband and wife about why they have bought some products twice or the colour of the loo roll . . . The tension increases and they come to blows. The checkout girl doesn't know what to do and looks at the floor. They use the opportunity to whisk through a rucksack full of shopping.

Forget this tactic. Most checkout girls today love domestics and won't miss a moment – unless you go so far as to tear each other's clothes off (but that technique might attract too much attention).

The secreter

This customer puts a blank CD in a box of Camembert, batteries inside packs of Coke cans, etc. All products which could be used to 'cover' others are well known by checkout girls. You'll either need more imagination or you'll need to come with a shopping bag with a false bottom. By the way you can also forget the 'Oh, I didn't see it!' excuse when the checkout girl discovers the booty . . .

The outraged customer

This customer is going out with his shopping when the security alarm sounds. Immediately he cries, 'It's a scandal! . . . Unbelievable! . . . You can't treat me like a thief when it's daylight robbery in this supermaket! . . . The alarm must be broken, this happened last time too! . . . I'm never coming back here.' The customer is hoping to intimidate the checkout girl or the security guard so they won't ask to see his purchases and will just let him through, worn down by his shouting. Even if you can be really frightening, forget this tactic. It has been used to death.

The athlete

The athlete passes through the tills at the speed of light, a large item under his arm and takes everyone by surprise. You need to be extremely fit with a good knowledge of rugby tactics to avoid being flattened at the exit by the security guards.

The bar-code switcher

He will swap the bar code of the product he wants to buy for that of a cheaper product. Two drawbacks: today the labels with the bar codes are very difficult, almost impossible, to remove, and they break easily. And secondly, you are unlikely to get away with it. The checkout girl will notice if a pan costs the same as a packet of salt. Don't take her for an idiot – it's an error that could be your undoing.

Out of sight, out of mind

He queues like everyone else. The checkout girl thinks he's a normal customer who is quietly waiting his turn. But suddenly he leaves the queue and makes a dash for the exit, his bag full of shopping under his arm. By the time the checkout girl can react and warn security he is already home free. He counts on the passivity of the crowd and the checkout girl's weariness. Nice try, but it won't work. This tactic requires the security guards also to be very tired or else absent altogether. So you have to choose your time carefully and watch out for the security guards' break times. It can be a question of seconds.

I would also like to warn you about a final point: beware of other customers. Some are born to tell tales and won't hesitate to betray you to a checkout girl or to management. Honestly, I promise. So be careful when you steal in the aisles (and hiding a pan under your jumper isn't very discreet anyway!).

Some useful advice, I hope.

Good luck!

Supermarket raids? Don't push it!

I'M THE BOSS!

Did you think that when you were on the till you were alone at the helm dealing with the customers? Wrong. You're forgetting your boss – who has one eye looking out for you and one eye watching you.

But who is he or she? What do they do? What is their day like? And what is the best way for you to manage your boss?

There are nearly as many managers as checkout girls in supermarkets. Some will last a few days, others years. Each will have their own method, goals and principles.

The efficient boss

They have climbed the ladder, rung by rung, through

hard work and they certainly deserve their place. They fully understand the workings of the store and know how to solve problems. They will be there to help if you have a problem.

Your till breaks down. You call your supervisor (naturally).

'My till is stuck.'

'I'm on my way,' the efficient boss replies immediately.

Three and a half seconds later the door of the Office opens and your supervisor emerges with a telephone in one hand and a screwdriver in the other. 'Good morning!' he says with a big smile for the customer. 'I'll take care of this little problem, won't take a second.'

Yes, managers like that do exist, I've actually met some!

The eternally dissatisfied boss

Fear not – you will also meet some moody ones. They don't say hello. Want to try the same with your customers? (Oh, that's right, you can't, you're not a boss.)

You will also come across the moaners. When it comes to the sensitive issue of cashing up, these are the bosses who harass you, adding to your stress. And they don't see any more need to be helpful than they do to be nice.

'My till is stuck. I can't do anything.'

'Again? Bloody tills! And bloody checkout girls who don't look after their equipment,' followed by an unintelligible grumble.

One of their minions will arrive a few minutes later to reboot the till. While you wait you should tell the customer a few jokes to keep the bad vibes emanating from the telephone from reaching the customer.

The God boss

This one only thinks about his career, his progress and his personal goals. He forgets that staff under his command still have rights. His weapon? Excessive communication. He writes hundreds of memos – on targets, turnover and performance. He spells everything out for you. You'll almost feel involved in the running of the store – until your lovely boss reveals his predatory side.

If you say hello to the union representative and chat with him for a couple of minutes you can be sure that thirty seconds later the boss will ask you if you have a problem with authority . . .

If you need to change your hours because of a personal appointment you'd better agree to do overtime (unpaid and claimed back in lieu . . . six months later) the week before unless you want to attract the rage of the God boss.

And if you are unlucky enough to contest a truly unfair decision by the boss he will quickly call you to order with his unanswerable argument: 'I'm the boss!'

You've learnt your lesson, I hope. Otherwise, punishment! No, not like at school where you take a note home for your parents and write out one hundred times, 'I will never say no to my lovely boss again.' It's another kettle of fish here. The good news will arrive with your rota. You'll have been given particularly horrible shifts (closing time every day, oh joy) or a change of post. Oh, so you fancy working on the customer service desk? Well, apparently you don't smile enough so you won't be going there.

The worst thing is that your boss will think that this punishment will be good for you. You think it will just cause more conflict. Obviously you don't share his view of life (or the same goals) . . .

The boss who wants everyone to smile

This one relies on mystery shoppers. Customers who apparently report the good and especially the not-so-good behaviour of the cashiers (I told you that some customers are born to tell tales). And this boss is only trying to increase customer satisfaction. And his customers will be more satisfied if his checkout girls smile more. Is this your boss? Lucky you, because he will try to do his best for his employees, he will always be in a good mood (or nearly always) and might even lend you his support.

This is a rare species so if you have one, don't let him go!

You should know though that your proven stupidity will force you systematically to appeal to your boss or his deputy for anything which is not explicitly part of your duties (you won't even be able to remove an item rung up in error on your own). And the surveillance cameras will always be on you. They will dissuade you from stealing a couple of pennies, catching a little nap, blowing your nose in a customer's bread or picking your nose. And thanks to the latest modern tills your boss can follow your turnover in real time and 'turn you off' when he feels like it.

So you see how work makes you free . . .

YOUR CONVEYOR BELT:
FRIEND OR FOE?

The conveyor belt: just another part of your till? Much more than that. It is your friend! It is the first contact with customers and can prove to be a formidable ally. It has a few tricks up its sleeve to take revenge on those who treat you badly.

With the customer in a hurry who keeps throwing you looks of exasperation (it's your fault that the store is so busy) and who has emptied his trolley like he empties his bin, your conveyor belt (your friend) will jolt slightly. And splat, the box of eggs is on the floor and the bottle of wine falls and breaks and splashes his nice beige trousers. Hardly guaranteed to speed up the shopping process. And he'll have to wait for the cleaning service to do their job. Poor thing (if you must smile, at least be discreet).

With the customer on the phone who completely ignores you when you help him pick up his change, which has fallen on the floor (not even a thank you), your friend the conveyor belt will eat the bank card he forgot to pick up (too busy talking on the phone). Your customer will have to wait at least twenty minutes to get it back. Oh, *now* he wants to talk to you!

With the child who won't stop crying all the time his mother queues (that's nearly fifteen minutes), who sticks his tongue out at you and throws his chocolate biscuit in your face, the belt will trap his fingers. Well, he shouldn't have tried to stop it. It's not a toy. He'll cry even more loudly now, but at least this time you know why he's crying.

With the customer who takes his sweet time, who doesn't care that the store closed ten minutes ago (do you recognise him?) and who loads his shopping on item by item, the conveyor belt will speed up, resulting in disagreeably loud screeching noises. The noise will still be ringing in his ears even once he's returned home.

But with the really nice customer who says good morning with a big smile and arranges his items from heaviest to lightest with the bar codes facing the scanner (wow!), the conveyor belt will be touched and let out a sweet purr. And everything will run smoothly.

Sometimes, however, the conveyor belt will let you down entirely – whether the customer is nice or not. It will change sides and support the customer. It will advance without stopping and unload all the items like a dumper truck. Impossible to stop it because it will do it so zealously that your only recourse will be the emergency stop button (the big red button which only works every so often). The items will be damaged and so will you. And don't forget that the customer will hold you entirely responsible (well, of course!). You can settle the score with these ungrateful conveyor belts at the end of the day with the bleach cleaner (every small victory counts) . . .

You might also come across one which, fed up with turning for years and years, will stop for ever with a long and final rattle. A heart-rending cry will indicate that your friend has left you, letting you down in front of a tidal wave of products and customers who think the belt has only malfunctioned. They will cry, 'This always happens to me!' and push their items along with their hand, grousing and shouting at you because, of course, you are responsible for their misfortune. The conveyor belt will remain immobile though. Immovable. Inert.

You think I'm exaggerating? Just wait. In the end, some days your solitude and powerlessness in the face of disagreeable customers will be so great that the least relief, even a malfunctioning or capricious conveyor belt, will be welcome.

So, in the evening clean it with love and when you arrive in the morning give it a little pat. It will love you. And who knows, maybe one day it will eat a customer or the petulant section manager.

HOW TO HIDE YOUR FORTUNE

You will sometimes come across customers whose physique is the stuff of fantasy. And you will be surprised to find that you are imagining them naked, dreaming that you are massaging their feet (or possibly other parts of their anatomy). And then there will be others who you'd rather not think about but who will be generous enough to let you enjoy a glimpse of some very appetising parts of their body. They all have something in common: a terrible fear of being robbed, which makes them hide their cash somewhere warm about their person. Average age: any (there are paranoid people everywhere).

When the time comes to pay you will be lucky enough to get a close-up view of:

• Mrs Jones's ample, flaccid bosom and her grey bra (it must have been white once) where she has hidden her banknotes. All accompanied by a puff of eau de cologne or sherry (difficult to tell).

• Mr Smith's scrawny foot and holey sock where he hides his £50 notes. Drawback: an easily identifiable odour. Oh actually, maybe that's from the smelly cheese he's bought.

• Mr Thomas's rounded stomach. His little arms always find it very difficult to reach underneath his jumper to his shirt where he has hidden his money. And you can smell that he didn't have time to take a shower today (or yesterday apparently).

• You can't see anything but you can hear Mrs Rogers: 'Wait, I don't have enough money, I'll just nip to the loo.' And when you see her a few minutes later, triumphant, with her notes in her hand you refrain from imagining anything. You are just happy to take the money from her fingertips.

Yes, yes, I know: you can't be fussy about where your money comes from. Especially when you're a checkout girl.

I'M PAYING

Paying for your shopping – an obligation that customers would avoid if they could. But, as you will have found out, customers make the checkout girl pay every day, each in their own way. Sometimes, you even start to ask yourself whether perhaps you are robbing the customers, given the black looks and insults they throw at you. So you might be surprised to learn that some actually fight to pay. Yes, you read that right. They fight.

The scene below actually happened.

Two friends come to my till to pay for a CD.

CHECKOUT GIRL
£19.99 please.

They both get their bank cards out at the same time.

FRIEND 1
Let me pay.

FRIEND 2
No, I should pay.

FRIEND 1
You paid for the meal yesterday.

FRIEND 2
Yes, but last week you did.

FRIEND 1
Yes, but you bought me the concert tickets.

FRIEND 2
That was a birthday present, it doesn't count.

FRIEND 1
You gave me a DVD too.

FRIEND 2
Yes, but I'd promised to do that for ages.

FRIEND 1
I know but I'd promised to get it for you.

FRIEND 2
It doesn't matter, last year you invited me over to yours more often.

The checkout girl is starting to feel dizzy. But it's not over yet. Friend 1 takes advantage of Friend 2's last reply to put her card into the machine. Friend 2 grabs her hand, the card falls out and Friend 2 puts in her own. Friend 1 jiggles it and manages to remove it but doesn't have time to put her own back in. Friend 2 takes both her hands and stands in front of her. Friend 1 struggles violently and tries to reach the machine which . . . slides off its base, hits the till and falls on the floor. But it's still not over. Friend 2 uses the confusion to put a £20 note in the checkout girl's hand. Friend 1 is ready to tear her arm off to get it back.

CHECKOUT GIRL (*unsteadily*)
If you want to settle this, please do it outside. I don't want there to be blood.

They burst out laughing. And Friend 1 lets Friend
2 pay.

I think this little story reveals a quirk in our society.
Paying is apparently the only real proof of friendship
between two best friends. And it's often the same in love
. . . I pay therefore I am.

Don't hesitate to remind your customers of this.
They'll pay up more easily, you'll see.

OUT OF THE MOUTHS OF BABES

A child's view of the world is full of insight, candour, poetry and tenderness . . . Your heart will leap when you hear this kind of thing:

Little Richard (aged seven) asks you, after watching your till closely, 'Where's your bed?'

Little Nicholas (aged nine): 'Can you give me money too?'
   Because he has seen you give his mother her change.

Little Julia (aged six): 'Are you in prison?'
   Because your till looks more like a rabbit hutch than a supermarket till.

Little Rose (aged five): 'Mummy doesn't have any money to pay for her shopping. She can only give you a cheque.'

Because the previous customer paid in cash and the little girl's mother had explained that she didn't have any change.

All that is quite sweet and will make you smile. But when parents use you to scare their children, keep smiling (you have to) but you can put them right.

When you hear a mother tell her child, pointing her finger at you, 'You see, darling, if you don't work hard at school you'll become a checkout girl like the lady,' there's nothing to stop you explaining that it's not a profession for stupid people, that you'd rather do this than be unemployed and that you actually have a good degree. (Five years in higher education? Really?)

If you don't, you may find that afterwards children don't respect you or see you as a failure . . .

And I have news for all those self-righteous people: it's been a long time since a degree guaranteed a dream job. Today's graduates sometimes have no choice but to do less skilled work.

Dear parents, thank you for using us as the bogeyman to raise your children! But you need to update your ideas a bit.

CHECKOUT GIRLS: THE FAIRER SEX

People are always saying that:

- Little girls are just as intelligent as little boys (and even better at school and university).
- The records of female sporting champions are just as impressive as those of the men. And the queens of wrestling almost as well known as the kings.
- Women can be just as bossy, angry and rude as men.
- Boys are just as attractive, sensitive, courteous, frivolous and chatty as women.

And there's no lack of proof. So why do we continue to put up with:

- Seeing 'Checkout Girl Number' written on your cash box every morning?
- The guys always (or almost always) being sent to the aisles to lift and organise merchandise instead of the girls?
- The term 'checkout girl' being used every day but never 'checkout boy'?
- There being far more girls behind the tills than boys?
- Our society still being eminently sexist?

It is true though – and I'd forgotten this – that, probably to shut up chronic moaners like me, retail has invented a very sweet term, 'checkout operator'. The debate is therefore closed and the problem solved, right?

I dream of the day when all checkout assistants, customers and managers are treated equally whatever their sex. We can all dream, can't we?

'YOUR TILL IS ON A BREAK'

There will come a time when you have to tell a customer, 'It's closed.' And they will almost certainly reply, 'But I've only got one item.'

The first few times you'll let yourself be convinced and scan their sandwich, electric drill or low-energy light bulbs. But very quickly you will learn to refuse politely (since there will always be others behind complaining that they too only have one item). Because, yes, even checkout girls have the right to take a break and relax for a few minutes.

So why is a break such a big deal? In your office if you want to leave your computer to go to the loo, have a coffee or chat for five minutes with a colleague, you don't need to ask permission. But you do on the till. It's like being back in primary school.

Want to say hello to a colleague in an aisle at the other end of the store? No, not possible during your working hours.

Need to nip to the loo? Have you asked permission?

Want a coffee? Have you begged for it?

Need a smoke? Has your request been accepted?

It's 1 p.m. and you're hungry but you've only worked half your six-hour shift. You need to ask before you can take your lunch break.

In retail (on the tills at any rate) that's how it works. You were hired to work on the till so you can't leave your post without permission. So whatever your request or the emergency, you have to make a telephone call . . .

Does it feel frustratingly as if you're being treated like a child (especially having to ask to go to the toilet!)? Get used to it.

And whether it's a little local shop or a big super-market, the procedure for asking for the right to leave your till is the same. You will engage in this little question-and-answer game on the telephone:

'Can I take my break?'

(Tick the relevant response.)

'Yes.'

'Someone will come and cover for you.'

'We'll ring you back, too many people are on their breaks at the moment.'

'Wait a little while, there's a rush on at the tills.'

Depending on the answer, your smile or grimace will reveal your state of mind.

And sometimes when they tell you, 'We'll call you back,' they might actually forget. You ring back forty-five minutes later (because you support the right of the other girls on the tills to take their breaks) and the answer may well be once again, 'We'll call you when you can take your break.' You'll be seething inside but won't be able to let that show in front of the customer who hasn't done anything wrong . . .

Another fake smile and off you go again.

There's another awkward moment for many checkout girls when they have to ask permission to go to the bathroom . . .

Imagine the scene: the store is packed and you have been squirming in your chair for two hours, improbably hoping that your need to go to the loo will disappear because you don't want to bother anyone. Unfortunately, the need remains and, after a while, you have to decide to ask to close your till while you relieve yourself. You pick up the phone and try to be discreet with regard to the customers who don't need to know that your bladder is full, all the while continuing to scan packs of loo roll and slices of ham.

After several attempts (the line is always engaged) someone finally answers.

'Can I leave my till for a second?' Trying to talk quietly.

'Why?' In an irritated tone that doesn't bode well.

'I need to go to the toilet.'

'Um, can you wait a bit?' (Choose the appropriate phrase.) 'You can take a break in an hour.' / 'You only went a couple of hours ago.' / 'But you only started your shift an hour ago!'

'But it's an emergency.'

'. . . Ummm' (or another muttering noise) 'someone will come and cover for you.'

(And in that case all you can do is hope that your replacement comes quickly!)

In some stores codes are put in place to allow you to make a request more discreetly on the telephone because being able to say 'Code purple', 'Can I have a 157', 'The sun is shining' or '1945' is more cryptic.

Because really not everyone wants to hear 'I need to go to the loo' . . . and you won't find customers' little smiles very amusing either.

It's complicated relieving your bladder when you're a checkout girl.

But let's get back to the subject of 'breaks'. It's a good day today, you've asked to take your break and your request has been granted. You'll even have time to go to the staff room!

But what's it like, this place where all the store's employees meet during the day? This room is the object of all the desires of the checkout girls, where they can leave their work and their customers just for a while. So is it nice?

Well, there are several kinds of staff room, ranging from kitchens (all the perks: table, chairs, fridge, fresh coffee, microwave) to dining rooms (no meals served though) with large tables and benches (narrow ones usually). Rustic, I grant you.

In big supermarkets, though, the room is designed differently. Here there is no fresh coffee for staff but an automatic coffee machine (not free obviously), machines with chocolate and sandwiches (they're not free either) and, if you're lucky, a water fountain (that's free, just cross your fingers that there are some plastic cups left). There are a few tables and chairs. But avoid taking your break at the same time as everyone else because seats are rare. As if everyone wanted to eat at the same time (how dare they!). And then there's the queue to heat up your food in the only microwave (it's a luxury if there are two).

It's a convivial room where the only decoration is an information board (messages from Health and Safety, the management, the union, adverts, etc.). In a corner are a few magazines to browse through, the same ones as six months ago.

But it would appear that it's not the same for everyone. I have been told (I would have loved to see it) that in other big supermarkets there are armchairs and a television (still no decorations though and the paint is peeling).

But apart from having a coffee and eating a sandwich, what happens in this room? That's easy, people chat! About everything and nothing, working conditions, relations with other employees and the bosses. Basically, it is a place to exchange information and set the world to rights. But look right and left first to check that there isn't a boss in sight or a manager who might overhear. You want to moan about people but you don't necessarily want the people involved to hear you . . . anyway, it all happens very quickly because with only three minutes' break for every hour worked (in some companies the break is longer: four minutes per hour!), you don't really have the time to talk for hours.

Let me set the scene (stopwatches at the ready).

Six hours' work? Lucky you, you get eighteen minutes' break.

You clock off, go to the locker room to get some change to pay for your coffee/sandwich/ bar of chocolate: two minutes gone (the corridors are long and you have to go upstairs).

You go to the bathroom and wash your hands: three minutes.

You go to the staff room: one minute.

Already six minutes gone; you've got twelve minutes left.

To save time you have got used to staggering your eating time with your break or eating cold food to avoid waiting until the microwave is free (so you save two to five minutes), which means you have a good ten minutes to enjoy your break.

Once you're settled, you flick through an old magazine which has been lying on a table for a few weeks. You are beginning to know the articles by heart.

A colleague arrives.

The discussion begins, you talk about working hours, break times which are too short, your last customers ('Can you believe it? He changed the label of the chrome coffee machine but he's a bit stupid. It's obviously worth more than £3!'). You talk about your families too, your holidays ('Is the boss going to grant me my week's leave?'), plans for evenings out and the lack of time you have to spend with your children . . .

One eye is still on the clock. People laugh. Another colleague arrives and already your eighteen minutes have almost run out. Your coffee has been swallowed quickly (did it burn? Too bad, you don't have time for small sips!), the last mouthful of sandwich is stuffed down and you have to go and clock on again quickly if you don't want to go over your break time (and be scolded by the boss). You've one minute left (barely time to go downstairs) before the end of your break.

You leave your colleagues and rush off. Your stomach is a bit heavy, you clock in and return to your till and customers are already following you, ready to jump on you as soon as the till opens.

Three minutes for every hour worked. It's a good way to learn how to manage your time and make the most of every minute. A checkout girl must be organised!

DO YOU HAVE 10 ITEMS OR LESS?

Yippee! You have been put on the '10 items or less' till.
A quiet day then. If I were you, I wouldn't get too excited.
10 = 10? Not on your till. Good luck!

10 = 20

CHECKOUT GIRL
Hello, do you have ten items or less?

CUSTOMER
Of course!

Number of items on the conveyor belt = 20.

CHECKOUT GIRL
Could you please go to another till?

CUSTOMER
You're just lazy!

10 = 11

CHECKOUT GIRL
Hello, do you have ten items or less?

CUSTOMER
Um . . . one, two, three . . . eleven, is that OK?

CHECKOUT GIRL
Eleven isn't ten.

CUSTOMER
You're not going to kick up a fuss about one little extra?

CHECKOUT GIRL
Ten means ten. But if you want, you can pay separately or remove one item.

CUSTOMER
Bloody hell!

10 = nobody

CHECKOUT GIRL
Hello, do you have ten items or less?

CUSTOMER
There's no one else here, you could take my trolley!

CHECKOUT GIRL
Sorry, this till is reserved for customers with less than ten items.

CUSTOMER
Bloody hell!

10 = 5 × 10

CHECKOUT GIRL
Hello, do you have ten items or less?

CUSTOMER
I've got about forty items but I'll pay in five different transactions.

CHECKOUT GIRL

Very clever. I'd never have thought of that.

10 = 10 × 10

CHECKOUT GIRL

Hello, do you have ten items or less?

CUSTOMER

No, a hundred but it's only ten different things. It's just that I've got ten of each.

CHECKOUT GIRL

That's OK then.

Yup, ten of one particular item only counts as one.

10 = come on!

CHECKOUT GIRL

Hello, do you have ten items or less?

CUSTOMER

No, but I never stick to that rule. I work at Discounts R Us and the checkout girls there let me through all the time.

CHECKOUT GIRL
Yes, but this isn't Discounts R Us, it's Fresh Goods
R Us!

CUSTOMER
Come on!

Being taken for an idiot, insulted, having to argue all the
time, getting involved in controversy, never giving in,
being intransigent, etc. So does the '10 items or less' till
still tempt you? Didn't you say that you had the begin-
nings of an ulcer? Just the place if you want to develop it.

PRIORITY? DID YOU SAY PRIORITY?

The sun is shining. Little rabbits are gambolling joyously in the fields. Peace reigns across the world. And mankind lives in perfect harmony where everyone is respected.

A utopia? In your world rabbits don't gambol and they're not smiling. Well, that's just not fair . . .

You are at a priority till. You must give priority to people in wheelchairs, disabled people, pregnant women and people with young children. It's essential to keep reminding yourself because you will be faced with several other 'priority' customers, all with a very good reason to be there. Never has the word 'priority' been used so often.

Priority customers:

- The customer who is desperate for the loo.
- The customer who has been up since five o'clock that morning.
- The customer who is three weeks pregnant.
- The couple whose favourite TV programme starts in five minutes.
- The mother with three children over eight.
- The customer who has flu.
- The customer who has a dinner party for eight people to organise.
- The father who has to pick his son up from nursery.
- The young woman who is late for her class.
- The customer who hates queuing (yes, they do try to claim priority).

And if someone who really has priority is waiting, you will have to convince the fakers to give up their place – and when they do agree, some will sigh loudly.

Rarer, and at the opposite end of the spectrum but just as surprising, is the very old man who gives you his disability card to prove that he isn't lying. If only everyone were like him . . . you'd be bored.

Wait till you find yourself confronted with this

situation: two elderly people, both in bad health, arrive at the same time at your till. Who should go first? How can you decide? The one whose arthritis is worse? A piece of advice: let them sort it out. The most belligerent will win. You can be nicer to the second one.

Don't let yourself be intimidated. Send fake 'priority customers' to other tills. That's what they are there for.

And no, the rabbits aren't smiling. I promise you.

CAN I SEE SOME ID PLEASE?

You thought that asking for ID for certain purchases was a formality that everyone would accept. How naïve! You will discover that for some people showing ID poses a problem; it affects their own sense of identity.

Yes, ID will give you intimate information about your customer. And maybe he doesn't want you to know his age (he looks much younger), his address (he's paranoid), his place of birth (he is ashamed of coming from Pratt's Bottom), her maiden name (she's ashamed of her father's name, Smellie) or maybe he's afraid that you will see his ID photo (he had a lot of acne then). So don't be surprised if you hear this kind of thing:

'What are you, MI5?'
(. . . no, the CIA.)

'But I'm thirty!'
(. . . and you want me to take your word for it?)

'You're joking!'
(. . . and the customer leaves without his shopping.)

'Really? No one's ever asked me for that before.'
(. . . OK, treat me like an idiot.)

'No need, I know your boss!'
(. . . and my sister knew the Beatles!)

To some people asking for ID is a capital offence and they will get really angry and insult you when you refuse to let them purchase their whisky. And be ready to duck because they might throw their shopping in your face (even when it's electronic equipment). They're above the law, no doubt. Or on the run from the law maybe. Crazy at any rate (if they pay with a credit card admittedly the checkout girl doesn't get all those details, but her boss does).

Others will show you some ID belonging to their friend or grandmother. The photo is a bit of a giveaway.

Yup, those customers have really got the point.

'Well, what's the difference? And, anyway, my friend was here just a couple of minutes ago.'

'Can't you ask her to come back?' Bizarrely, you didn't see the friend.

'She's gone.' Getting agitated, 'For God's sake!'

And the customer leaves you her shopping and rushes off.

In any case, never give in (even if you find them very attractive). If there's ever a problem, particularly with an overseas cheque, your management will be quick to tell you that 'you didn't do your duty as a checkout girl' and make you pay. Be an incorruptible checkout girl! (But you can laugh inside when you see Mr Jones's face when he was twenty on his driving licence or that Mr Smith was bald two years ago on his ID card and today it's visibly no longer the case . . .)

BLESS YOU!

Notice for Staff (following several complaints from customers)

Checkout girls, do you have a cold? Please stay at home. Even if your doctor can't sign you off work because your cold is benign, stay at home anyway, you plague-stricken person! Why? Because you touch customers' items with your hands, which are covered in germs, and you might sneeze at any moment and 'blow your nose on their bread'!

Do you have a cold because customers are forever sneezing and coughing all over you? So? The customer is king. They have a right to give

you their bugs but they do not want to get
yours.

Enjoy your time off.

The Management

£19.99 PLEASE!

Beeeep!

CHECKOUT GIRL
£9.99 please.

The customer hands you a £10 note. You give
him a penny in change and bless the inventors of
such tricksy prices.

£9.99 instead of £10.
    £19.99 instead of £20.
    £99.99 instead of £100.
    'That's a good deal! Quick, let's buy it! Life is cheap!'
So say consumers every day.

You can also thank these inventors for all the wonderfully fulfilling moments you will have.

Instead of spending ten minutes cashing up, you will spend fifteen because of all the 1p, 2p and 5p pieces you will have been given during the day. And your fingers will be covered in a thin layer of copper mixed with . . . dirt.

More than fifty times a day you will have to answer the following questions and respond to the following remarks:

CUSTOMER
£19.99? Couldn't you just say twenty?

CHECKOUT GIRL
Well, no. My job is just to tell you the exact amount to pay.

CUSTOMER
Can't you round it up?

CHECKOUT GIRL
I'm not in charge, talk to the management.

CUSTOMER
Keep the change!

CHECKOUT GIRL
1p, how kind! But we're not allowed to accept tips,
however small and generous they are.

CUSTOMER
I'm fed up with all these little coins in my wallet.

CHECKOUT GIRL
Save them for charity.

CUSTOMER
I'm 1p short, can't you let me off?

CHECKOUT GIRL
Sorry, I'd like to but it's not possible.

. . . yes, it works both ways.

Not forgetting that 'Nineteen-ninety-nine-please' takes
nearly twice as long to say as 'Twenty-pounds-please'. At
the end of the day the time lost must represent about two
or three fewer customers served by the checkout girl. If I
ran a supermarket, I'd be worried.

News Update (rumour and gossip)

According to the latest news, the Bank of England has run out of small coins. Too many people are keeping them at home in jars or piggy banks (how sweet . . .). They might be removed from the market. Yippee! Rejoice, dear customers, the prices might be rounded up one day.

MY TILL, MY LOVE

Did you think that once you were in the swing of things life on the till would be easy? You and your till are one, your gestures automatic, you no longer have to think, and you neither hope for anything nor fear anything? Be careful! A terrible danger awaits you: management could choose at any time to send you to the till at the petrol station to cover for a colleague. And then, panic! You will be completely lost.

In order to stop the shock being too violent and to prepare you psychologically, here are the main tests that await you.

A till that is completely different from the one you're used to, customers who want to buy a bottle of camping gas,

128

who come and complain because the petrol pumps aren't working, who beep their horns like crazy people because you are too slow, who poison you with their exhaust fumes . . . Above all, don't be overly polite, they hate that.

Customers 1 – Checkout girl 0

Are you trembling? It's not over yet. You will witness moments straight out of disaster films:

Everything was quiet that day but the arrival of a young man at breakneck speed changed everything. He tore into the petrol station at 100 miles an hour, stopped at the pumps and took down a fire extinguisher.

'Hey, he's stealing it!'

Incredulously I jump up. He notices me. Stopping in his tracks, he points in a particular direction. I look over and notice with horror a parked car with its bonnet open and flames coming out of the engine just next to the bottles of gas (a perfect parking place).

Panic! The only thing I can think to do at the time is call security. By the time they arrive the driver has contained the fire. And all the while customers continue to fill their petrol tanks . . .

Customers 2 – Checkout girl 0

Don't worry, you will also see great spectacles (theft, hold-ups etc.), and violent scenes (two drivers grabbing each other because neither wants to give way).

Customers 3 – Checkout girl 0

Just a word on what to do when these things happen: don't give in to panic and call security straight away (and if you are keeping score, do it discreetly).

Beg and plead not to be sent to cover for a colleague the day before the start of the holidays or long weekends. You might not survive that ordeal. Between the pumps, the noise of the cars, the screaming children and the insults of customers rushing to drive 500 miles, the struggle will prove to be particularly difficult and unequal.

Customers 4 – Checkout girl 0

Ah yes, the life of a checkout girl is full of unexpected events and dangers. So, a piece of advice: don't rest on your laurels. Vigilance should be your watchword.

On the other hand, one advantage awaits you at the petrol station. You will have your own personal loos (with a door) only a few feet from your till (including a flush which leaks and smells). Isn't life great?

Customers 4 – Checkout girl 1

And there are other reasons to celebrate your trip to the petrol station. If you survive the experience you will have lots of stories to tell your friends and, in particular, once you're back at your till in the store you will think you're in paradise. The insults, fights, horns and hold-ups will be nothing but far-off memories.

NB: I advise you not to read the following, particularly if you have been feeling fragile recently. But I feel obliged to write it. It would be profoundly dishonest of me to stay silent about . . . the other disagreeable surprises that await you.

When you become a checkout girl you should understand that you risk having to work:

On the customer service desk

At the entrance to the store. This is not as complicated as you'd think. You just have to find a few good arguments to shut up customers who come to complain that one of your colleagues didn't want to give them a bag, the music is too loud, the prices are too expensive, the meat counter is not properly signposted or stocked (there's no Welsh lamb), there are too many customers, etc. Nothing too complicated, you see. Of course, you will also need to master all the subtleties of refunds, exchanges and organising loyalty cards. Child's play really . . . after several weeks of effort and a smile for every challenge . . . if all goes well.

On the credit desk

I can't find the courage to describe what awaits you if ever . . . in short, your mission will be to get your customers into more debt. But if ever you manage to do it you will be bursting with pride for the rest of your life. You will feel a bit as if you work in a bank.

In the Office

The great privilege of this post is that you will have practically no contact with customers. Nice, huh? The disadvantages: answering the phone, having to count the money in the safe and using the computer to find the bar codes of items when the checkout girls don't have them, preparing rotas and knowing how to answer any question that comes your way in three seconds. Not for everyone, I know. Especially if the computer gets stuck . . . but that never happens . . . well, almost never . . .

At the culture and/or multimedia centre

The good news is that this doesn't exist in all super-markets. More good news: if it does, the customers are very nice (they almost all say hello and smile) and sometimes ask you for advice. No need to panic. You just have to tell them if the latest Coldplay album is better than the last Oasis one, the latest Bruce Willis film better than the last Harry Potter, the last Harry Potter book better than the latest John Le Carré. OK, giving your opinion is exactly the opposite of what is required of a checkout girl and you'll need courage, time and a few brain cells to listen to, watch and read a few new releases in this area (don't be too zealous about it though). But if you manage it, euphoria will light up your life and you will miss your till a little less.

That's a fairly exhaustive summary of the dangers which lurk. Keep calm. And, I should have said this at the outset – sorry, what was I thinking? – these posts will only be occupied by checkout girls who request them and who are really motivated. Management only uses the best ones (the ones with degrees or who are regularly No. 1 on the league table . . . or however it is they judge. It all depends on your manager).

However, there is another kind of promotion (generally short-lived). With a bit of luck and real skill (that your store will be happy to use when it needs it), you can get yourself a proper job: you can work in the aisles or work in the Office to replace someone who's on holiday for a few weeks or months (accident, maternity leave, long-term sick leave, etc.). You'll love that. Finally, you get to leave the till to do something you like. But don't rest on your laurels – when the person you are replacing comes back, there's no chance of keeping the post that you liked so much . . .

These replacements will never last for more than a few months. To be clear, fewer than 5 per cent lead to a permanent post (yup, hurrah, career development for checkout girls in supermarkets is close to zero – heaven forbid that you might actually be given some responsibility). So when it's the turn of other girls to replace someone, you won't have any reason to be jealous. They won't be paid more than you and won't change status. 'Till assistant' will continue to be written on their pay slips. And if they look down on you a bit during the replacement period, once they're behind the till again they will go back to being the checkout girls they always were.

OK, you can breathe easy again. In the end it's more frightening than dangerous. But the petrol station? Sorry, that threat is very real, even if you never ask for it. So be aware!

By the way, have I mentioned the self-service tills (more profitable than even the most badly paid checkout girls) which might replace you altogether one day? We'll talk about that when you're feeling better.

GAME OVER

Have you been working for a few hours non-stop? Do you feel tiredness coming over you? Careful! You are soon going to experience the 'Little Beep Moment', a great moment in your day. Let yourself go and embrace this unreal minute.

The store is very busy. Trolleys are bumping into one another in ever greater numbers, the wheels grinding and creaking. All around you harried customers come and go incessantly. The loudspeakers crackle out the latest special offers and the background music becomes insistent.

The ambient noise is getting more and more unbearable. Your maximum threshold has almost been reached. All that's needed is one more loud noise and you'll be tipped into another dimension. It's the yelling of a child that does it. For about sixty seconds you exist in a parallel universe.

The noise, the conversations, the music . . . it all stops. Customers, colleagues, the entire supermarket disappears. Now there are only the beeps of the till in answer to those of the neighbouring till. And suddenly you feel like a match is on, as if a virtual tennis ball were going back and forth between you and your colleague. You're playing Pong!

Then, after that furious game, it's on to Breakout, the famous game with bricks. Your hands are the paddles and the items are the balls that you have to send to the other side of the till without them falling over or, worse, bouncing off other products. If that happens an enemy ball might appear, as dazzling as it is effective (if the customers agree to play!) . . . But in general it's OK. The levels are quite easy! The only real problem is when the shopping makes a 3D brick wall.

Then comes the final boss (the big monster at the end of the level) which irredeemably appears at the time of payment. And there you have to be quick. To beat him don't forget to shoot him with his loyalty card and whatever payment method the boss uses and finish him off with a 'Goodbye-thank-you', accompanied by a glittering smile.

But be careful because some bosses have secret

weapons like Unreadable Cards or Unreadable Cheques.

Sixty seconds later and the muffled sound gives way once more to the usual noise.

You have just experienced what I call the checkout girl's 'Little Beep Moment'. It generally happens when you have passed your six thousandth beep of the day. Sometimes, too, you will become Pac-Man (chased by ghosts, endlessly consuming the same little dots) – generally, after your three thousandth 'swallowed' item.

DID YOU SAY BAR CODES?

Who said that your job as checkout girl was monotonous? Don't forget the customers. Thanks to them the days follow on from one another but are never the same. They will never cease to surprise you.

Like the one who came to my till without any items, just a list in his hand. He gave it to me and I saw that he had scrupulously noted the thirteen-figure bar codes of all the items he wanted to buy (about twenty of them). Here, I said to myself, is a customer ahead of his time. Did he hope that by the time I had scanned his bar codes an employee would be outside in front of his car with his order ready? Or did he expect home delivery? Or had he applied the principle of 'large items can be collected at customer service' to all items in the store so as to be more practical?

I never knew. When I refused to scan them he replied, irritated, 'I always do it like this!'

Really? Sorry but I don't work in a cyber-supermarket. Give me their address and I'll apply though (think about it – a piece of paper is much lighter than a family pack of beer!).

And just so you don't live your whole life behind the till without knowing, this is what the figures under the black bands on the bar codes mean. The standard is thirteen digits (for very small objects there are only eight). The first two or three figures indicate the country of the company's headquarters (from 300 to 379). The subsequent numbers give the family, product brand and any other information needed to codify the item. The bar code is unique for every kind of product. Now you'll never scan another bar code in the same way, right?

STRANGELY STICKY

One day you may be fortunate enough to come across this guy. He looks really nice. He says hello and even smiles. And he puts his shopping down on the conveyor belt properly.

Ten out of ten!

I scan his yoghurts, bottle of wine, ham, cheese and packet of crisps . . . and feel something sticky.

'Strange,' I say to myself in passing, 'no jam or honey coming up.'

After putting the packet down, I have a look at my fingers, curious. I notice a small, indefinable substance. I look more closely, rubbing my fingers together. I still can't identify what it is. I stretch it, it's elastic and remains stuck to my finger. Then I get it – it's a nose bogey! Yes, how nice of the customer to give his checkout girl such a gift. Would you like a packet of tissues with your crisps?

I had a lot of trouble getting rid of it. It was really very sticky.

DRUNK CUSTOMERS

Drunk customers will never fail to astonish you. They are never short of ideas or ridiculous arguments. You will find them quite fascinating.

Whether it's the one who asks you if you have a corkscrew to open the bottle of wine he has just bought.

Or the one who falls head over heels in love with the first customer he sees in the aisle and pursues her across the store, his can of beer in hand.

Or the one who thinks he's Father Christmas and generously distributes the store's products to customers.

The one who drinks a whole bottle of extra-strength lager there and then (well, maybe he's thirsty and the soft-drinks aisle is too far away).

The one who falls in love with you in the beer aisle

(what were you thinking of, returning the six-pack of Stella a customer left at your till fifteen minutes earlier?) and declares his passion with pauses for hiccups, releasing bad breath which could knock you over.

Or the one who is so drunk that you wonder how he found the supermarket and the alcohol aisle in the first place (a sixth sense undoubtedly). But it's difficult to walk and avoid things which are suddenly in front of you: a trolley, a pack of water (dreadful stuff!) on the floor, a pile of loo-roll packs (good Lord, why create a Tower of Pisa? And he barely touched them (for which read, he tripped over them) and they fell all over the floor) . . .

It's hard work being thirsty.

THERE WILL BE BLOOD!

Did you think that, despite the insults and the way people look through you as if you weren't there, your store would actually be quite a civilised place? Don't you believe it! When I tell you that working in a supermarket means seeing all sides of humanity, I really do mean all!

Screams. A chase through the shopping centre. A security guard and a man exchange blows. The first onlookers stop – and contemplate the scene. The man calms down. The security guard holds him firmly by the arm. They move away. Fisticuffs break out again. People, more and more of them, surround the unexpected scene. The fight becomes more violent, the blows harder. The people stand in a circle watching the street fight in the shopping

145

centre. Men, women, children, bags and trolleys mingle. It takes three security guards to overcome the madman.

Curiosity. Voyeurism. The bloodier and more obscene, the better. Hey, look! Blood is pouring out of the security guard's nose. Wait until I tell everyone about this!

The guards try to take the man to a quieter place. The crowd follows. The guards move away again but only manage to take a few steps before the man flies into a rage once more. Is he to blame? Or is he the victim?

Four men have had a violent fight. There are at least thirty spectators but no one reacts. And there are just as many employees open-mouthed in front of this spectacle. It's the same with accidents in the street, everyone watches but no one (or very few) reacts. The brawl ends with the arrival of the police, who take away the troublesome customer.

Once the show is over and the last curious people have left with their shopping (with the final scenes playing merrily in their heads), only the security guard remains. He wipes away the traces of blood – the last vestiges of a fight in an improvised ring.

The moment of madness has passed – a moment when man reverted to his instincts. And you, you remained behind your till, unable to react.

J'ACCUSE

When you accepted the post of checkout girl you thought that you wouldn't learn anything except the essentials of your wonderful job. How wrong you were! You are in a perfect position to witness the entire range of human stupidity – and you will be delighted to know that it is limitless. It's enough to make your mouth water.

Saturday, 8.30 p.m.: You have scanned the shopping of 350 or 400 customers (a good day). They have mostly been nice and some even very nice (they greeted you when they were on the phone). Your hearing is starting to go back to normal. The supermarket compere promoting the 'special offers on beer' finally shut up a few minutes ago. Your conveyor belt is like new. You

147

have cleaned it with love. Your bin is closed properly. No pieces of paper or crisps are lying around. The store is almost empty. All you have to do now is take your cash box proudly back to the Office. You tell yourself that, for a Saturday, it could have been worse. To celebrate you start to whistle your favourite song (or whichever one has been played twenty times through the loudspeakers that day). Then two blokes arrive at your till carrying three bottles of beer.

CHECKOUT GIRL (*pleasantly*)
It's closed, I'm afraid. You'll have to go to the till over there. That one's free. (*She points to an open till a few feet away.*)

FIRST MAN (*unpleasantly*)
Come on, you can take us. We've only got three bottles. It's the Beer Special, for God's sake!

CHECKOUT GIRL (*firm but telling herself that she should have been less zealous in cleaning her till*)
Sorry, it's closed.

FIRST MAN
I'll give you £1 – then you can take my bottles!

CHECKOUT GIRL (*still firm but thinking that she would really like a security guard to turn up*)
No thank you – it's closed.

SECOND MAN (*very pleasantly*)
Come on! Checkout girls are like whores! When you offer them a tip they always say yes! Take our bottles, you whore!

The checkout girl is now wishing she were Arnold Schwarzenegger so that she could (repeatedly!) knock the heads of those two idiots against her very clean till while telling them, 'Enjoy your beer specials, idiots!' You can always dream.

Stupidity appears to be the most widespread of human traits, so I have some advice to stop you getting depressed: buy yourself a punchball.

CAN YOU GO TO THE NEXT
TILL PLEASE?

How can you annoy a customer legally?

It requires special organisation. You are about to open but you have gone to find a free chair (yes, again). Your colleague, two tills away, is just getting settled (she has a chair) and between the two of you stands an empty, closed till (without a chair).

The customer (preferably in a bad mood) arrives at your colleague's till. She is far from ready (what a lazybones!) and sends him to you. He lets out a sigh. He doesn't see you (you are still looking for your chair) and thinks your till is the one just next door to your colleague's. He waits for you. Another sigh. You return with your chair (finally!) but behind him so he still doesn't see you.

Two customers, who have been following you, leap on your till. At the same time your colleague warns the customer (the one who's waiting) that you are behind him. Another sigh and he says, 'She could have told me that she wasn't here!' Another sigh. He heads to your till where a third customer has just arrived. Another sigh. You have started to scan the items of your first customer. Another sigh . . . and another and another.

Your colleague indicates that she is open (sorry, her till is open) so you tell him, 'My colleague has just opened. You can go to her till.' The customer lets out yet another sigh and a stream of expletives, abandons his basket and leaves, disgusted. Poor thing. Checkout girls can be so disorganised!

We'll play again tomorrow, I promise.

WILL IT SCAN OR WON'T IT?
THE SIX STEPS FOR GETTING PRICES

You are in your trial period. You want to be hired at any price. And when you got up on this Saturday morning, you decided that you wanted to be the best checkout girl of the day. This evening your number (not your name! Don't push it!) will be at the top of the Office till league table. A nice challenge! (Though I must remind you that to encourage you management will pay you not a single penny extra for this victory.)

You started an hour ago and you are keeping up a very good pace. You decide to speed up a bit when suddenly, *beeeeep!* On your till screen you see 'unknown product'. Yes, you know what that means: the item in your hands won't scan. And if you don't know the price you're stuck.

Don't panic.

Step 1: Enter the numbers on the bar code. Still nothing? That's normal, there was only a 1 per cent chance that it would work (still, it was worth a try).

Take a deep breath.

Step 2: Call the Office. Line engaged? Bad luck. Wait and smile at your customer, who is starting to lose patience . . . Finally, someone answers!

CHECKOUT GIRL
The price for Andrex extra-soft loo roll please, the code isn't going thr—

OFFICE (*interrupting*)
I'll send someone over.

Wait again (I know, what fun), tell your customer (who is starting to go red in the face) that someone will be there in a second, and tell those behind him to go to another till (if not, I warn you you'll get sighs and shouts within thirty seconds).

And on to Step 3 . . . a good five minutes later: the 'runner' has arrived (finally, but hard to blame it on him when you know he has to handle thirty tills all by himself). You immediately give him the packet of loo roll. The runner (a new employee) asks where to look. Oh dear! You want to send your customer to help him but you decide not to. He is crimson by now.

Quick, on to Step 4: Tell a few good jokes to your customer to make him relax and to make sure he stays (he might want to go, leaving you with all his shopping). Don't be afraid to use your secret weapon: 'I have a mini-bar under my till. Can I get you a drink?' He smiles, it's working. The runner is back already with the price and your customer has seen him too. Incredible! (You're not so unlucky after all!)

Quick, Step 5: Call the Office to register the item, its bar code and its price on the central computer. The computer's crashed! Don't lose your cool now, only a 'few' seconds to wait. And smile, it's not your customer's fault.

Step 6 and . . . nine minutes later: *beeeep!* OK, the super-soft loo roll has gone through.

So you lost fifteen minutes and nine customers? Your place as No. 1 is severely compromised. Never mind, you'll win next Saturday. Or you can make up time during your break.

Oh goody, a Bargain Hunter has come to your till. It's definitely not your lucky day.

ROLL UP, ROLL UP:
IT'S SALE TIME

The first day of the sales: an important event in the life of the organised consumer who wouldn't miss it for anything. And also for the checkout girl (even a blasé one). It is a new opportunity to delight in being at work and not on holiday on a desert island.

8.25 a.m.: The Opening Time couples, the morning crazies, the Bargain Hunters and 'all the rest' can be counted in their dozens. Never before will you have felt so strongly that war has been declared or, if you watch too many horror films, that zombies are attacking.

There won't be enough to go round today so have no pity! No scruples about shooting people killer looks, pushing and walking over one another without apology (don't leave your feet lying around all over the place then!), being rude to each other (me first!), growling (is there a dog here?), using trolleys like assault tanks – and good for you if you run over someone's foot (fewer competitors).

8.55 a.m.: You arrive at your till and swallow a yawn. You anxiously observe these dogged customers and prepare yourself psychologically for their relentless consumerism. It's going to be a busy day.

9 a.m.: The wild animals are let loose. May the best (or the most aggressive) win!

Everyone heads for the technology aisle to get a good deal on a flat-screen TV. The people who came the day before to do some research are the first ones there. Too heavy?

'Never mind. Sit on it, darling, while I go and pay for it. And bite or hit anyone who tries to take it!'

The DVD players are also going like hot cakes.

'£30? A bargain! I'll take the last three.'

'They don't have the remote control. You can't navigate through the menus of your DVDs without it.'

'Never mind, a bargain is a bargain.'

And the clothing aisle, so lovingly organised by the employees before opening time, has become a real battleground in barely quarter of an hour. Has a customer found the *very* dress she was looking for? She has grabbed it out of the hands of another girl who had just taken it off its hanger, knocking over a pile of jumpers in the process. Never mind, it is the *very* dress she was looking for. She beams a winner's smile and continues her search in the aisle. But suddenly, what has she seen just over there? The *actual very* dress she was looking for. What should she do? Drop the first one on the floor like an old cloth. The sales assistants can pick it up. That's what they're paid for. And grab the *actual, very, only* dress she ever wanted. Is it much too small?

'Never mind, I'll go on a diet tomorrow.'

Further along, a customer has grabbed the woollen sock of his dreams, green with nice sprawling octopuses. Is the other one missing?

'Never mind, I'll upend the box to find it. Too bad if most of it goes on the floor. It will be easier for other customers to find what they want. Are people walking all over the socks? Who cares?'

9.10 a.m.: Over to you, dear checkout girl. It's an emotional moment, the first compulsive shoppers at the till. You will be surprised (even if nothing surprises you now) at the number of items sold by your store, items of whose existence you were not even aware (even though you've been working there for several years). It's a parade of unsold and unsellable, useless items. The waltz of the sales *beeeep* begins.

Sometimes, a little lucidity (what am I actually going to use that for?) or guilty conscience (I'm already £800 overdrawn) or both will make customers abandon some of their great bargains at the last minute. So don't grumble if you find barometers in the shape of rolling pins, solar alarm clocks (without batteries), enormous cow-shaped slippers (with udders), granny knickers and shovels without handles in the chewing-gum display at the end of your till. After your day's work go and put them back in their aisles ready for the next sales. It's a chance to stretch your legs after a whole day sitting at your till.

And more than any other day you will feel that you have become a refuse collector. Most of your customers will confuse your conveyor belt with a bin and literally upend their trolley or basket. It's your job to take each item and sort through their mountain of bargains as quickly as possible. Few customers bother with politeness – too much of an effort for today. Luckily, you might be able to count on your friend, the conveyor belt. Its jolts will make the pile of garden gnomes, flower-pot holders and planting trays fall over and will easily swallow a few little pairs of knickers and some T-shirt sleeves (oh bother, it's all ripped and it was the last one too).

You are well trained but be prepared to see the same scenes over and over again throughout the day:

'Is that the reduced price? I think it's a bit expensive!'
    'Yes. I check each time that you have been given the reduction.'

'The price isn't on it but it was £1.'
    'I'll call to check.'
    'If you must! But you're making me late.'
    An aisle assistant arrives with the actual price: £15.
    'Really? As much as that? That's not what I saw. I don't want it.'

You will also have to call your supervisor (with a smile and in good humour) at least twenty times to cancel purchases. Some customers will have been a bit too quick to believe that the sales won't actually cost them anything. Apart from misers, it's not the wealthiest people who come that day. Wealthy people don't need to shop in the sales. It's those on low and middle incomes who come to exact their revenge for the normally high prices and to prove that they too have the right to consume. The sales are a good way of making people who don't actually have any money spend it anyway.

The first day of the sales is an ideal opportunity to get a good look at the personality of the twenty-first-century consumer. It is an exceptional day that any checkout girl worthy of the name must experience at least once in her life (and more if you enjoy it). And if some of the complexities escape you on the first day, you have six weeks to get to grips with it. The twenty-first-century consumer will no longer hold any secrets for you.

Have you missed the sales period? Don't worry! After that there are special offers, stock clearances and other one-off sales. The year will be full of bargains!

THE WEEKEND SHOW

Do you still want some excitement? Have you been hoping to show the world that checkout girls can still be their own person, or nearly? With a good dose of self-sacrifice and a bit of luck you could experience this kind of situation.

It's Saturday afternoon, it's raining and there are lots of people hanging around the store. I am standing in for a colleague at the vouchers desk (yes, another post checkout girls can find themselves occupying). A man arrives in a suit and tie. He buys about ten vouchers. We chat for a few minutes while I process his request and print his vouchers. When the time comes to ask him how he wants to pay, he gets out his cheque book. I have to tell him, 'I'm sorry but you can't pay for vouchers by cheque.' I show him the notice on the counter indicating the accepted payment methods. 'See, says so there.'

'But no one told me before!' he retorts.

Having experienced this kind of misunderstanding before (it happens a lot) and in order to calm things down quickly, you phone the Office to ask for confirmation. The customer can then see that you're not talking rubbish (after all, you're just a checkout girl).

So I call the Office and ask, 'You can't pay for vouchers by cheque, can you?'

'No, you can't,' comes the reply.

I hang up the phone and turn to the customer, repeating (yes, sometimes you turn into a parrot) that no, you can't pay by cheque. He won't drop it though.

'Call your supervisor, I want to see her.'

'Of course, I'll ask her to come.'

I pick up the phone again. 'It's me again. Could you come and explain to the customer why he can't pay by cheque?'

And at the end of the line I hear an apologetic voice: 'No, that's not possible at the moment, I'm on my own here and the boss is already sorting out a problem at the till. You'll have to deal with it.'

Irritated voice: 'Oh . . . I'll see what I can do.'

I hang up and turn to the customer, attempting to smile.

'Sorry, but my supervisor is already busy with a customer. She can't come and talk to you.'

The customer goes very red. He starts shouting (so that everyone can enjoy the situation, how generous of him) and gesticulating. Although I try to remain unruffled, I also end up raising my voice because by now I've had enough.

We are apparently here to serve.

We have to show them respect.

But being shouted at for something you can't change and you can't control, no . . .

Suddenly we are into a nice argument. He shouts. So do I. He yells. Customers covertly approach so they don't miss anything. A show – how exciting! . . . Well, it's not every day that you hear a checkout girl and a customer arguing at full pitch!

Our 'discussion' is doomed to failure though, since neither of us will give in. After several unpleasant minutes (shouting is fun in a football stadium but not so much at the till) I notice an aisle supervisor out of the corner of my eye. What luck! Given the noise, he must have heard. He'll definitely come over and calm things down. But my hope is short-lived. He acts as if nothing has happened and changes aisle . . .

The customer finally gets out his bank card. With an abrupt gesture he flings it at me. It falls on the floor. That makes me even more annoyed but I pick up his card, give it to him and say calmly, 'Sir, I refuse to serve you. You've gone too far and I won't be treated like that!'

'. . .'

The argument ends abruptly. The man apologises, pays for his vouchers and leaves.

Ten minutes later one of the girls from the Office finally arrives. She has come to see whether I have been able to handle the argument. I describe the brawl and she tells me, 'Go and take your break. Someone will replace you.'

Do you need the support of a superior? *The number you have rung is not available.*

Are you sure that you are handling a situation properly? *Careful, you are only a checkout girl.*

Do you want to serve people? *I repeat, you are only a checkout girl.*

And the moral of the story? A few days later the rules are changed. You can now pay by cheque. OK, it's not exactly a moral but why should there be one?

THE BIG CHRISTMAS RUSH

Ah, Christmas! A period of festivity and sharing? Frankly for you, dear checkout girl, 24 December involves exactly the same stress as the first day of the sales. It's all about quick execution, increased scanning, big crowds, grumbling customers, empty aisles, compulsive shopping, even more impatience than usual . . .

Welcome to the spirit of Christmas! I know, it's horrible but if you really want to enjoy the season to be jolly, avoid this job.

24 December, morning. The same old story. War has just broken out and the zombies are attacking. Customers are buzzing like flies in front of the store doors (which open at 8.30 instead of 9 a.m., an important distinction).

With the same fear of missing out, they leap not on the technology and clothes aisles but the fish/meat/dessert aisles. They're stocking up for the big blow-out tomorrow. But you will feel the same aggressive atmosphere as at sale time. Perhaps it's a foretaste of the dyspepsia to come.

'It's a shame we can't serve ourselves. We'd have the turkey, sausages, smoked salmon, bacon, beef and Christmas pudding in the trolley already and we wouldn't have to yell at the idiot who pushed in front!'

From 9.15 a.m. onwards the same generalised chaos reigns in the aisles as at sale time. The sales assistants are on the verge of a nervous breakdown the same as at sale time. Not for the same reasons, it's true. This time it's because some customers can't understand why the most popular toy of the moment might be out of stock on Christmas Eve and kick up a fuss (thirty-six of them simultaneously). Others only want to give big gifts (nice ones!) but for less than £5. Others still don't have any idea what they want to give. It is up to the sales assistants to spend two hours looking for them (and they'd better find something good!). There are also those who arrive three minutes before closing and who still haven't made their mind up, when the lights go out (darkness isn't great for choosing what colour plates to buy).

And of course at the tills you find the same cordiality and politeness as normal but worse . . . Today truly there are only bad offers to be had. All the prices have gone up for the event. And it's obviously your fault. So you can read in their furious glances: 'You expect me to pay an arm and a leg, you don't want a thank you as well surely!' and/or 'You're not the one who has to cook this turkey so hurry up, you stupid bird.'

But don't forget to keep smiling sincerely even when they shout at you for the fiftieth time that day because you can't wrap presents or because you haven't provided a nice piece of ribbon to hide the horrible colour of the packaging, which – what bad taste – includes the store's logo! 'It's not very Christmassy, your hideous packaging!'

And you must wish them Merry Christmas and Happy New Year as you give them your nicest smile. And you will have to repeat at least 350 times, about five times more than normal, 'Yes, I check each time that you have received the reduction.'

Actually, the comparison between Christmas and the sales is not accurate. The decorations (multicoloured tinsel and plastic Christmas trees vs special-offer posters screaming '50% off') are quite different. You might be wearing a Father Christmas hat on 24 December. For the sales you will be wearing a goblin hat. In both cases though you will look ridiculous (and the glamorous or grandma outfit won't help . . .)

Another important difference to bear in mind is that on Christmas Eve your store will close at 7 p.m. instead of 10 p.m. (as it does on the first day of the sales). Yes, but you can be sure that you will be just as tired and at the end of your tether.

And when the doors finally close and you think that you can breathe again, don't be surprised to see a frustrated consumer getting heated and yelling, 'Let me in! I have to buy a present!'

'We're closed, madam,' the security guard replies.

'What? But that's not possible, I can't go home without a present!'

'We're closed, madam,' he will repeat several times.

You are allowed to laugh (inside). If necessary, you can defend yourself by saying it was nervous laughter . . .

And don't forget that most of the presents chosen with care, or not, by your customers will end up on websites at half price on Boxing Day . . . OK then, Christmas is a bit like the first day of the sales after all.

Happy Christmas, enjoy your supermarket dash and be sure to be up at the crack of dawn on Boxing Day to be first online for the best bargains . . .

COUNTDOWN

Saturday, 3 January: my last day. No, it's not a dream!

All the familiar gestures and words I've repeated tens of thousands of times . . . today will be the last time. I can't believe it! I'd like to sit down to think about it but . . . I have to work. ('Just because it's your last day doesn't mean you're being paid to do nothing!')

I arrive at the Office and say hello, as I do every day (they actually answer this morning). It's the last time I will look at the board to find out my hours and which tills I'll be working on: Till 12 until 3 p.m., Till 13 until 9 p.m. – oh joy, next to the freezers all day! And I forgot my scarf!

As usual I glance at my cash box and check whether I have enough coin rolls for the day. Yet again, I ask for

£1 and £2 coins. I take a few sheets of paper towel (just in case a packet of crisps breaks, a bogey gets stuck to my fingers, a customer needs to blow his nose after sneezing on me or another of life's pleasures) and leave the Office.

I only have a few hours left working for this company. I won't feel the same about the customers I meet today. Do I have regrets? I wouldn't go that far . . .

11 a.m.: Clocking-in time. No chair . . . as usual. But this time I get one in less than five minutes (better late than never!). And immediately I hear, 'Are you open?'

'. . .'

And for the first time I don't answer (I don't care!). The customers (my last three hundred!) parade past, one after the other. Amongst them are some of my favourites: the customer on the phone, Mr Smith with his holey sock and his smelly foot, the Bargain Hunters, the customer with his embarrassing loo roll, the 'Where are the toilets' customer. Some very nice ones too – no, not the customer on the phone who remembers to say hello – but ones who have read my articles on the website, who wish me luck and promise to treat checkout girls like human beings from now on. Hurrah! That's a great leaving present (so I haven't wasted my time).

8.45 p.m.: Announcement that the store is about to close. Already? The day has gone really quickly. It's all the emotion, I expect.

8.55 p.m.: My last customer.
'Don't you have any bags?'
It's always nice to end with a classic.

I glance at the aisles to check that the Closing Time couple aren't nearby. No – what a shame! I would have treated them like kings this time. Never again would they have come to do their shopping at 8.55 p.m.!

The day is over. I clean my conveyor belt with particular care ('I'm going to miss you, you know. Thanks for helping me so much') and the rest of my till. It is all so automatic that you almost forget why you're doing it. This evening though, I know that it's for the colleague who will take my place tomorrow. I wonder who will replace me on this till? You don't normally think about that. Why should you?

Last check. Last look from this side of the till. Everything is in order, nothing is lying around. With my cash box under my arm I walk down the line of tills one final time to the Office. The white tiles seem to continue endlessly in front of me. My feet are taking the same path that they have followed almost every day for the last few years though. It is difficult to tell myself that the next time I come here I will just be a customer. I slow down. I want to keep a bit of my soul here.

The security shutters come down. The blinding white fluorescent lights are turned off and we are left in the shadows. My footsteps resonate in the great empty store. A solitary *beeeep!* can still be heard like a goodbye from the tills I used all these years. But it's time to go to the Office and cash up for the last time.

The amount is correct! It's strange to think it's the last time I'll handle all those coins and notes. The money is returned to my cash box and I close it for the final time. It is given to my colleagues in the Office. The label with my number will soon be taken off the metal box and given to the person who will replace me.

Who will then become just a faceless number.

Checkout girls are often only temporary. They are employees who come and go and one looks much like the other . . . or do they?

A little glass of champagne? Orange juice? Some goodbye crisps at least? Dream on. You were a checkout girl, remember, not a lawyer! My colleagues hug me. It's a good thing they're there.

I clock out one last time (well, I hope so!). 9.15 p.m. Right on time. Ah, that capricious machine which made me enter my card over and over again. This time I win! Someone else will be using this card tomorrow.

Employees come and go and one looks much like the other . . . or do they?

I think that the tills will haunt me for a long time. The lights, the background noise, the familiar faces of all the customers I met over the years, all the colleagues I worked with. All that is over for me today. Eight years behind the till (amazing!). I leave with a big (recyclable) shopping bag full of memories and *beeeep, beeeep, beeeep* . . .

So do you still want to be a checkout girl? Is it still your dream job? No? I didn't think so! But do you have a choice? No, I didn't think so. Good luck anyway. And then, if it's really terrible, do what I did and write a book. And who knows, maybe it will be sold in supermarkets for . . . £6.99. Keep the change.

ACKNOWLEDGEMENTS

Thank you to all the colleagues who helped and supported me and made me laugh over those eight years on the till, and particularly those who have become real friends.

Thank you to the first readers of my blog who gave me a reason to keep going and put it down on paper.

Thank you to Iris and François who helped me so much with my writing.

Special thanks to Liliane, my eagle-eyed proofreader, for her excellent advice.

Thanks to my family who are always supportive and who pushed me to fulfil my ambitions.

And finally, and above all, thank you to Richard, my husband, for always being there.

The first Victor Legris Mystery

MURDER ON THE EIFFEL TOWER

Claude Izner

(Translated by Isabel Reid)

The brand-new Eiffel Tower is the glory of the 1889 Universal Exposition. But one sunny afternoon a woman collapses and dies on this great Paris landmark. Can a bee-sting really be the cause of death? Or is there a more sinister explanation?

Enter young bookseller Victor Legris. Present on the Tower at the time of the incident, he is determined to find out what actually happened.

In this dazzling evocation of late-nineteenth-century Paris, we follow Victor as his investigation takes him all over the city. But what will he do when the deaths begin to multiply and he is caught in a race against time?

'Isabel Reid's seamless translation captures the novel's many period charms' **Independent**

'. . . a clock-beating thriller . . . entertaining views of nineteenth-century Paris' **Financial Times**

'. . . a charming and amusing whirl around a time of rapid social and intellectual change' **Morning Star**

'Reading Izner is like taking a ride into the belle epoque in a time machine. A wonderfully breathtaking ride' **Boris Akunin**

'The taut pacing and vivid period detail will have readers eagerly turning the pages' **Publishers Weekly**

ISBN 978-1-906040-01-7

£7.99

To purchase this title visit www.gallicbooks.com or call 020 7349 7112.

The second Victor Legris Mystery

THE PÈRE-LACHAISE MYSTERY

Claude Izner

(Translated by Isabel Reid and Lorenza Garcia)

On a wet March evening in 1890, Odette de Valois vanishes from the Père-Lachaise cemetery during a visit to her late husband's grave. Her maid, Denise, fears the worst and knows of only one person in Paris who can help: her mistress's former lover, Victor Legris

When the frightened girl turns up at his bookshop, Victor reassures her, certain there must be a simple explanation for Odette's disappearance. But as he begins to investigate he realises it is a far more sinister affair than he first suspected.

'. . . *brilliantly evokes 1890s Paris, a smoky, sinister world full of predatory mediums and a ghoulish public, in a cracking, highly satisfying yarn*'
Guardian

'. . . *briskly plotted, intriguing second outing for Legris*' **Financial Times**

'. . . *an extremely enjoyable, witty and creepy affair*'
Independent on Sunday

'*Terrific atmosphere, unusual, full of drama*' **Susan Hill**

'. . . *top Gallic hokum*' **Observer**

ISBN 978-1-906040-04-8

£7.99

To purchase this title visit www.gallicbooks.com or call 020 7349 7112.

The third Victor Legris Mystery

THE MONTMARTRE INVESTIGATION

Claude Izner

(Translated by Isabel Reid and Lorenza Garcia)

November 1891.

The body of a young woman is discovered at a crossroads on Boulevard Montmartre. Barefoot and dressed in red, she has been strangled and her face disfigured. That same day a single red shoe is delivered to Victor Legris's Parisian bookshop.

Suspecting more than just coincidence, the bookseller sleuth and his assistant Jojo are soon engaged in seeking out the identity of both victim and murderer.

In this third investigation set in *belle-époque* Paris, we are drawn with Victor into the city's nightlife and the legendary Moulin Rouge immortalised by Toulouse-Lautrec, who features in the story.

'. . . *conveys the fin-de-siècle atmosphere extremely well and Paris, with its leafy boulevards, its slums, cafés, railway stations and its night-life, is richly conveyed*' **Historical Novels Review**

'*Full of pungent period detail . . . a satisfyingly convoluted yarn*' **Observer**

'*A charming journey through the life and intellectual times of an era*' **Le Monde**

ISBN: 978-1-906040-05-5

£7.99

To purchase this title visit www.gallicbooks.com or call 020 7349 7112.